Plays of America
from American Folklore
for Young Actors

Smith and Kraus *Books For Actors*
YOUNG ACTORS SERIES
Great Scenes and Monologues for Children
Great Scenes for Young Actors from the Stage
Great Monologues for Young Actors
Multicultural Monologues for Young Actors
Multicultural Scenes for Young Actors
Monologues from Classic Plays 468 BC to 1960 AD
Scenes from Classic Plays 468 BC to 1970 AD
New Plays from A.C.T.'s Young Conservatory Vol. I
New Plays from A.C.T.'s Young Conservatory Vol. II
Plays of America from American Folklore for Young Actors 7-12
Seattle Children's Theatre: Six Plays for Young Actors
Short Plays for Young Actors
Villeggiature: A Trilogy by Carlo Goldoni, *condensed for Young Actors*
Loving to Audition: The Audition Workbook for Young Actors
Movement Stories for Children
An Index of Plays for Young Actors
Discovering Shakespeare: **A Midsummer Night's Dream**,
   a workbook for students
Discovering Shakespeare: **Romeo and Juliet**, *A Workbook
   for Students*
Discovering Shakespeare: **The Taming of the Shrew,**
   A Workbook for Students

CAREER DEVELOPMENT SERIES
The Job Book: 100 Acting Jobs for Actors
The Job Book II: 100 Day Jobs for Actors
The Smith and Kraus Monologue Index
The Great Acting Teachers and Their Methods
The Actor's Guide to Qualified Acting Coaches: New York
The Actor's Guide to Qualified Acting Coaches: Los Angeles
The Camera Smart Actor
The Sanford Meisner Approach
Cold Readings: Some Do's and Don'ts for Actors at Auditions

If you require pre-publication information about upcoming Smith and Kraus books, you may receive our semi-annual catalogue, free of charge, by sending your name and address to *Smith and Kraus Catalogue, P.O. Box 127, One Main Street, Lyme, NH 03768. Or call us at (800) 895-4331, fax (603) 795-4427.*

Plays of America
from American Folklore
for Young Actors

by L.E. McCullough

Young Actors Series

SK

A Smith and Kraus Book

A Smith and Kraus Book
Published by Smith and Kraus, Inc.
One Main Street, PO Box 127, Lyme, NH 03768

First Edition: March 1996
10 9 8 7 6 5 4 3 2 1

Library of Congress Cataloging-in-Publication Date

McCullough, L.E.
Plays of America from American folklore for young actors / by L.E. McCullough
p. cm. -- (Young actors series)
Summary: Fifteen original plays with themes taken from American folklore.
ISBN 1-57525-040-3
1. Folklore--United States--Juvenile drama. 2. Children's plays, American.
[1. Folklore--United States--Drama. 2. Plays.] I. Title. II. Series: Young actor series.
PS3563.C35297P58 1996
812'.54--dc20   96-1702
CIP
AC

Acknowledgements

The author wishes to thank the following for professional literary development and scholastic support:

Dr. Frances Rhome of Indiana University-Purdue University at Indianapolis; James Powell of the Writers' Center of Indianapolis; Tom and Yvonne Phelan of Pharaoh Audiobooks; Sean O'Sullivan of University College Dublin; Hugh Shields of Trinity College Dublin; Lee Gutkind of the University of Pittsburgh; Nancy Bogen of Twickenham Press; Nancy Kline, Director of the Writing Program at Barnard College; Robert Graham Small, Kathleen Tosco, Paul Hildebrand and the entire company of the 1995 Shenandoah International Playwrights Retreat—and—my wife, Kitty.

Dedication

Though I first came to formally study folklore at the Folklore Institute at Indiana University-Bloomington as a college undergraduate, my earliest interest in folktales came from my family—particularly two aunts, Catherine and Margaret Igoe, who during vacation outings at the New Jersey shore regaled me and my cousins with hilarious, terrifying ghost stories—and my parents, Isabel and Ervin McCullough, who on my fourth birthday made me a present of *My Book House,* an incredible series of story books edited by Olive Beaupré Miller that contained hundreds of folktales from around the globe, tales that inflamed my youthful imagination with an appetite for fancy and fantasy that has never abated. To them, and to all the other families throughout history who have passed down folklore to the next generation, I respectfully dedicate this book.

CONTENTS

The Author

L.E. McCULLOUGH, PH.D. is a playwright, composer and ethnomusicologist whose studies in music and folklore have spanned cultures throughout the world. Formerly Assistant Director of the Indiana University School of Music at Indianapolis and a touring artist with Young Audiences, Inc., Dr. McCullough has performed for elementary and high schools throughout the U.S. and has recorded with Irish, French, Cajun, Latin, blues, jazz, country, bluegrass and rock ensembles on 31 albums for Angel/EMI, Log Cabin, Kicking Mule, Rounder, Bluezette and other independent labels. Winner of the 1995 Playwrights' Preview Productions Emerging Playwright Award, his Celtic Ballet, *Connlaoi's Tale: The Woman Who Danced On Waves,* received its world premiere with Dance Kaleidoscope in March, 1995; his book of original stage monologues, *Ice Babies in Oz,* was published in April, 1995, by Smith & Kraus, Inc.; his stage play, *Blues for Miss Buttercup,* debuted in New York in June, 1995. He is the author of *The Complete Irish Tinwhistle Tutor* and *Favorite Irish Session Tunes,* two highly acclaimed music instruction books, and has composed filmscores for three PBS specials—*Alone Together, A Place Just Right* and *John Kane.* Since 1991 Dr. McCullough has received 35 awards in 26 national literary competitions and had 178 poem and short story publications in 90 North American literary journals. Dr. McCullough is a member of The Dramatists Guild, Inc. and the American Conference for Irish Studies.

FOREWORD

It's always seemed to me that legends and yarns and folktales are as much a part of the real history of a country as proclamations and provisos and constitutional amendments. The legends and the yarns get down to the roots of the people — they tell a good deal about what people admire and want, about what sort of people they are.

—Stephen Vincent Benét (1898-1943)
American poet and short-story writer

I'm the yaller blossom o' the forest! I'm half horse, half alligator and a mite touched with snappin' turtle! I can lick my weight in wildcats, hug a b'ar too close for comfort and wade the Mississippi! I'm a ring-tailed roarer, and I can out-dance any critter on land or sea or sky! Now, let's get on with this frolic, for I'm just gettin' warmed up, and I'm rarin' to go!

—Davy Crockett (1786-1836)
American congressman, soldier and folk legend

•

The ten plays in this book are drawn from the seemingly bottomless, ever-evolving fount of American folklore and popular culture. They range from European, African and Asian folktales recast in New World settings to the mythology associated with real-life figures such as Abraham Lincoln, Mother Jones, Johnny Appleseed and Elvis Presley and actual incidents in United States history. Put them all in a pot, stir with a generous portion of salt and spice and you've got a succinct, savory sample of America's folk heritage ready for instant staging!

Many people today mistakenly believe that "folklore" is nothing more than weird stories about make-believe people in bygone days—

fairy tales, Jack and the Beanstalk, Mother Goose, haunted houses and so forth. In fact, folklore has for centuries served as a major source of inspiration for some of the greatest musical, literary, dramatic and artistic works ever created, from symphonies, ballets and Broadway plays to movies, paintings and Pulitzer Prize-winning novels. Even as you read this sentence, folklore based on our own contemporary world is taking shape, coloring our perception of what we experience in the present and how we will be perceived by future generations looking to the past.

Folklore has always fulfilled an important educational function in human society, from earliest times to the present. Folklore transmits information about how the world came to be, providing concrete answers to the infinite variations of the question relentlessly posed to adults by children everywhere: "Why?" Folklore describes the group's accepted behavior standards—and what might happen if these standards are violated (*taboo*). Folklore communicates crucial knowledge about work, family rearing, warfare, worship and recreation. Far from being a collection of cultural leftovers or silly nursery stories, folklore is a distilled, superbly expressive synopsis of a group's shared history, social order and moral belief system.

Episodes from the living drama of American history have been extensively used by American playwrights, from the nation's revolutionary beginnings to the present. *The Fall of British Tyranny* or *American Liberty Triumphant* by John Leacock of Philadelphia galvanized popular sentiment for George Washington's troops when it appeared in 1776; since then thousands of plays have invited audiences to celebrate our shared social and political history, ranging from George L. Aiken's adaptation of *Uncle Tom's Cabin*, Dion Boucicault's *The Octoroon* and Frank Hitchcock Murdoch's *Davy Crockett* to 20th-century works such as John Wexley's *They Shall Not Die*, Arthur Miller's *The Crucible*, Jerome Lawrence and Robert E. Lee's *Inherit the Wind* and Robert Schenkkan's *Kentucky Cycle*.

The *Plays of America* series has been designed to combine with studies in other disciplines: history, costume, language, dance, music, social studies, etc. If you are a music teacher and want to add some more Mississippi River flatboat songs to *Annie Christmas and the Natchez Trace Bandits*, go ahead and make it a class project. *Johnny Appleseed and Willie Crabgrass* can supplement lesson plans in environmental awareness and preservation. If your class is doing *Les Flammes d'Enfer* in conjunction with an area study of the southern United

States, feel free to have the characters speak a few additional lines of French and decorate the set with bayou architecture and plants. Each play has enough real-life historical and cultural references to support a host of pre- or post-play activities that integrate easily with related curriculum areas.

Besides those youngsters enrolled in the onstage cast, others can be included in the production as lighting and sound technicians, prop masters, script coaches and stage managers. *Plays of America* is an excellent vehicle for getting other members of the school and community involved in your project. Maybe there is an accomplished performer of gospel music in your area; ask them to teach some additional spiritual numbers to the cast of *When People Could Fly*. Perhaps someone at your local historical society or library can give a talk about early American labor history for *The Most Dangerous Woman in America*; a geology enthusiast could add details about 19th-century mining operations for *The Seven Chan Brothers of Paiute Pass*. Try utilizing the talents of local school or youth orchestra members to play incidental music…get the school art club to paint scrims and backdrops…see if a senior citizens' group might volunteer time to sew costumes…inquire whether a restaurant might bring samples of Chinese cuisine for *The Seven Chan Brothers of Paiute Pass* or Cajun food for *Les Flammes d'Enfer*.

Despite the fanciful nature of many of these plays, each is rooted in a historical or cultural reality that tells us much about the people who created it. Though the plays encompass a wide span of ethnic groups, time periods and geographic locales, each ultimately is concerned with some virtue or failing common to all humanity — cleverness and bravery in the face of danger, the foiling of vanity and greed, loyalty to family and friends, respect for the world we must all inhabit. While these works should not be viewed as "morality plays," they can serve as starting points for discussion about contemporary ethical and social issues of relevance to teens.

Most of all, have lots of fun. Realizing that many performing groups may have limited technical and space resources, I have kept sets, costumes and props minimal. However, if you do have the ability to rig up an entire Illinois courtroom for *Abe Lincoln for the Defense* or build a facsimile hold and main deck of a 19th-century steampacket ship for *The Splendid Voyage of Kitty Doyle*—go for it! Adding more music and dance and visual arts and crafts into the production involves more students and makes your play a genuinely multi-media event.

Similarly, I have supplied only basic stage and lighting directions. Blocking is really the province of the director; once you get the play up and moving, feel free to suit cast and action to your available population and experience level of actors. When figuring out how to stage these plays, I suggest you follow the venerable UYI Method—Use Your Imagination. If the play calls for a boat, bring in a wood frame, an old bathtub or have children draw a boat and hang as a scrim behind where the actors perform. Keep in mind the spirit of the old Andy Hardy musicals: "C'mon, everybody! Let's make a show!"

Age and gender. Obviously, your purpose in putting on the play is to entertain as well as educate; even though in the historical reality of 1858 an American courtroom jury would have been all male, there is no reason these roles can't be played in your production by females. After all, the essence of the theatrical experience is to suspend us in time and ask us to believe that anything may be possible. Once again, UYI! Adult characters, such as grandparents or "old mountain men" or "bearded fiddlers," can be played by teens costumed or made up to fit the part as closely as possible, or they can actually be played by adults. While *Plays of America* are indeed intended to be performed chiefly by students, moderate adult involvement will add validation and let teens know this isn't just a "juvie project." If, in a play like *When People Could Fly*, you want to get very highly choreographed or musically intensive, you will probably find a strategically placed onstage adult or two very helpful in keeping things moving smoothly.

Integrating authentic ethnic or period music is a great way to enhance your production. If you have questions about where to find recordings or written music of the tunes or genres included in these plays, or want some tips on performing them, I would be happy to assist you and may be reached in care of Smith & Kraus, Inc.

The *Plays of America* series offers the opportunity to learn a little bit more about all of us who make up this amazing nation called the United States of America. And for some adults perhaps, these plays might recapture the joy and excitement we all felt the first time we heard a thrilling tale of pioneer valor or frontier derring-do. Who says you can't be a kid again? Just put on this coonskin cap, pardner, and meet me at a little spot in San Antone called the Alamo...

L.E. McCullough, Ph.D.
Woodstock, New York

JOHNNY APPLESEED AND WILLIE CRABGRASS

Johnny Appleseed is a legendary figure in American folklore, a true American original. He was also an actual person, born Jonathan Chapman in Boston, Massachusetts, in 1775 and spending more than forty years wandering the Midwestern frontier until his death in 1847 near Ft. Wayne, Indiana. It is estimated that he planted and cultivated fruit orchards throughout an area covering more than one hundred thousand square miles, teaching settlers how to improve their nutrition and agricultural methods. A gentle, peaceable man, he lived in harmony with Native American tribes and was a strong advocate of literacy, introducing books and the joy of reading into the lives of many illiterate frontier folk.

TIME: Yesterday, Today and Tomorrow

PLACE: Your Town, Your World

CAST:

Teenage Boy	Traveler	Teenage Girl
Traveler's Wife	Johnny Appleseed	Traveler's Boy
Willie Crabgrass	Traveler's Girl	Mr. Chapman
Mrs. Chapman	Homesteader	2 Shawnee Indians
Homesteader's Son	Settler	Settler's Boy
Settler's Wife	Settler's Girl	Neighbor with Cider Press

STAGE SET: a table with four stools; a park bench with a city trash basket; a log; a cider press

PROPS: two apples; 2 brown paper lunch sacks; several small apple seed pouches; burlap tote sack; 2 hoes; honey jar; wagon cart; torch; 19th-century revolver; cobbler's hammer; wodden clog; canoe paddle; pocket comb

SPECIAL EFFECTS: sound of bees buzzing

COSTUMES: Teenage Boy and Teenage Girl wear present-day teen leisure clothes; Willie Crabgrass: early 1800s dandy dress—vest, frock coat, top hat, cane; Johnny Appleseed and other 19th-century characters wear basic early 1800s pioneer dress; Shawnee Indians wear buckskin, moccasins, feathers

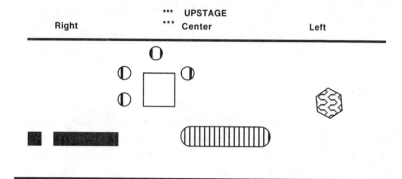

Stage Plan -- *Johnny Appleseed & Willie Crabgrass*

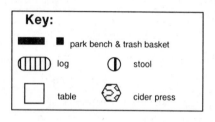

(LIGHTS UP STAGE RIGHT on a park bench where a TEENAGE BOY and TEENAGE GIRL sit, a foot or so apart, eating lunches from brown paper sacks. They munch without speaking, glancing furtively at each other when the other isn't looking. Finally, the BOY takes out an apple, polishes it and offers it to the GIRL.)

TEEN BOY: Uhhhh, would you, like, like an apple?
TEEN GIRL: An apple?
TEEN BOY: Yeh.
TEEN GIRL: That apple?
TEEN BOY: Yeh.
TEEN GIRL: Now?
TEEN BOY: Yeh!
TEEN GIRL: Sure. *(takes it, studies it)* Thanks. Hmmm. Williams Pride.
TEEN BOY: Huh?

TEEN GIRL: This apple. Williams Pride is the name of the genus. The *type*. Williams Pride is a sweet, medium-sized, dark-red variety. Matures in mid-to-late August. It's also immune to apple scab and other diseases, even when there's an excess of rain during the growing season.

TEEN BOY: Gee, that's impressive.

TEEN GIRL: What's impressive?

TEEN BOY: All that stuff you said about the apple. You're, like, a regular Johnny Appleseed or something.

TEEN GIRL: Well, I know about him.

TEEN BOY: Who?

TEEN GIRL: Who? Who you just said—Johnny Appleseed.

TEEN BOY: Oh, right. Me, too.

TEEN GIRL: Really? Tell me something you know about him.

TEEN BOY: Johnny Appleseed? Uhhhh, let's see…he wore a coonskin cap and stole apples from the rich to give to the poor. Annnnd fought at Pearl Harbor. Or something. What else is there to know about the dude? He was obviously psyched about apples. Hey, you wanna go to the Bongo Puppy Whistle concert Saturday night?

TEEN GIRL: *(turns away)* Not with somebody who doesn't know beans about Johnny Appleseed.

TEEN BOY: Yeh? Well, what do *you* know about Johnny Appleseed?

TEEN GIRL: *(turns to him)* First of all, his real name was Jonathan Chapman. And he was born in Boston in 1775.

(LIGHTS DOWN ON BOY AND GIRL; LIGHTS UP STAGE LEFT as JOHNNY APPLESEED enters and walks to center stage, stopping at the log; he carries a sack and sets it down next to the log.)

JOHNNY APPLESEED: Hello, friends! My name is Jonathan, Jonathan Chapman. You can call me Johnny Appleseed—most folks do. I was born in Boston during our country's War of Independence, the year they fought the Battle of Bunker Hill, as a matter of fact.

(JOHNNY'S parents, MR. AND MRS. CHAPMAN, stand stage left; she holds a baby; he points offstage left with his cobbler's hammer and a shoe.)

JOHNNY APPLESEED: My parents were ordinary folks, my father a shoemaker, my mother a seamstress. They were never rich, but they were always happy. They used their talents to make life better for folks, better in simple ways—a nice-fitting suit, a comfortable pair of shoes. And they took a great delight in the simple things of this world. Why, the first thing my baby eyes saw when they opened, was a beautiful branch of apple blossoms outside the nursery window waving in the gentle breeze.

(LIGHTS OUT LEFT; MR. AND MRS. CHAPMAN exit left; JOHNNY APPLESEED picks up sack.)

JOHNNY APPLESEED: When I was nineteen years old, I decided to go West and seek my fortune as a farmer. I traveled to Pittsburgh, which was only a tiny village then, deep in the Allegheny Mountains. I built a log cabin on a hill outside of town. There was a creek and good soil for oats and corn. And there was a pretty little grove of apple trees in back—a beehive, too. *(sits on log)* But when I wasn't busy in the field, I'd sit on my porch and watch the folks headed further West pass by.

(A Pioneer Family—TRAVELER, TRAVELER'S WIFE, their small BOY and GIRL—enter from stage left, pulling and pushing a wagon cart.)

JOHNNY APPLESEED: Hello, friends! Where you headed?

TRAVELER: We're headed to O-hi-o! All the way from Old Vermont.

JOHNNY APPLESEED: That's a mighty long way. Are you hungry or thirsty? Do you need a place to spend the night?

TRAVELER: Don't think so, but thanks anyway.

(SOUND: BEES BUZZING, FADE UNDER AFTER 10 SECONDS.)

TRAVELER'S WIFE: Why, look children—look at all those bees! Careful now!

PIONEER BOY & GIRL: Bees! Lookit all the bees!

TRAVELER: By golly, mister, you've got quite a hive!

JOHNNY APPLESEED: *(picks up a jar)* Would you like some honey? I've got a big jarful, and it's awful sweet.

TRAVELER: Well, that's right friendly—

TRAVELER'S WIFE: Amos, no! We have to save our money for the ferry across the Allegheny.

PIONEER BOY & GIRL: Pleasssse! Pleasssse can we have some honey! Pleasssse!

TRAVELER: Hush, now! You heard your mother. We don't have money to spare on candy!

JOHNNY APPLESEED: Why, folks, you don't have to pay me for this honey. Here. *(hands jar to TRAVELER'S WIFE)* After all, the bees don't charge me anything for it; why should I charge you?

(They all laugh; JOHNNY takes a small pouch from his pocket and stands.)

JOHNNY APPLESEED: And here...these are some seeds from my apple grove out back. Why don't you take them for your farm in Ohio?

TRAVELER: *(takes pouch)* Thank you, stranger. Thank you kindly.

(The PIONEER FAMILY exits right; JOHNNY sits on log, rests his head in his hands on his knee and closes his eyes; SPOTLIGHT ON TEEN GIRL AND TEEN BOY, SITTING STAGE RIGHT.

TEEN GIRL: Johnny had a dream that night. He dreamed he was on his front porch watching a whole parade of settlers headed West pass by. And in his dream, he gave each one of them a pouch of apple seeds to plant on their farms. After awhile, the whole country was filled with beautiful farms and apple orchards.

(JOHNNY wakes up, smiles and walks to stage left where A NEIGH-BOR stands turning a cider press.)

TEEN GIRL: He went to his neighbors and asked them for the ground-up mash left in the presses when they made apple cider. Then he went home and spent all winter picking out the seeds from the mash. He dried the seeds, sewed them into little deerskin pouches, and when spring came, he went to the waterfront and gave away the pouches to folks headed West.

(JOHNNY passes out seed pouches to SETTLERS mime tips his hat, waves.)

TEEN GIRL: Pretty soon, people forgot his last name was Chapman and just called him Johnny Appleseed.

(SPOTLIGHT OUT ON TEEN GIRL AND TEEN BOY; JOHNNY sits down on log with a puzzled expression.)

JOHNNY APPLESEED: The more I got to thinking about it, I knew there was a problem with my idea of just giving out apple seeds. You can't just throw seeds anywhere and expect 'em to grow into orchards overnight! They have to be nurtured and cared for, like any other living thing. It was a big job, but I knew the person who had to do it.

(He picks up a canoe paddle and starts rowing; LIGHTS UP STAGE LEFT on a HOMESTEADER and HOMESTEADER'S SON clearing a field with hoes; the SON sees JOHNNY APPLESEED and stops hoeing.)

HOMESTEADER'S SON: Hey, Pa—who's that man in the canoe?

HOMESTEADER: *(looks at JOHNNY, squints, chuckles)* Why, son, that's Johnny Appleseed. *(waves at JOHNNY, who continues to row)*

HOMESTEADER'S SON: The man who gives away apple seeds?

HOMESTEADER: That's him. He's been traveling the Northwest Territory since 1801, planting apple orchards everywhere he goes. I believe he's paddled up every creek and river for a hundred thousand square miles, from the Ohio to the Maumee and back—all the way to Indiana and Kentucky, even Lake Erie. There's not a settler in the territory isn't glad to see Johnny Appleseed!

(JOHNNY disembarks from canoe, steps ashore, begins sowing seeds, tending to an orchard.)

HOMESTEADER'S SON: How does he do his planting?

HOMESTEADER: Well, he finds a nice spot by some fresh water and clears away the underbrush. He plants the seeds, then builds a fence to keep deer from nibbling the first shoots. Then he gets back in his canoe and heads to the next orchard.

HOMESTEADER'S SON: Where does he sleep at night?

HOMESTEADER: He sleeps out in the open, son. He lives on berries and apples and roots and cornmeal mush; he doesn't favor killing animals for food. Why, he doesn't even carry a gun and or knife. And some folks says he can talk animal language.

HOMESTEADER'S SON: Animal language? What do you mean?

HOMESTEADER: *(chuckles)* One night Johnny Appleseed crawled into a hollow log; unfortunately a big old grizzly bear had the same idea— and arrived there first. Johnny settled down, laid his head down on something soft and furry, but Mr. Bear—he woke up on the wrong side of the bed, so to speak. Well, Johnny and the bear had a conversation about the situation. Johnny apologized to the bear, backed out of the log and found another place to sleep down the way. The bear didn't lay a paw on him.

(Two SHAWNEE INDIANS enter stealthily from stage right; they see JOHNNY, watch him, then go up to him and shake hands enthusiasti-

cally; all three sit in a circle and talk, display seed pouches, mime plant-ing motions.)

HOMESTEADER'S SON: Well, isn't Johnny Appleseed scared of Indi-ans? Those Shawnee can be might fierce.

HOMESTEADER: The Indians think he's a powerful, wise medicine man. He knows as much about the woods and nature as they do; in fact, he even showed them new ways to plant and grow corn. Back during the War of 1812, when the British had the Shawnee fighting on their side, Johnny got wind a lot of settlers were going to be attacked. So he ran all through the countryside, warning every family he could find to go to Fort Mansfield for safety till the trouble had passed.

(INDIANS and JOHNNY exchange handshakes; Indians exit left be-hind HOMESTEADER and SON.)

HOMESTEADER'S SON: And the Indians let him do it?

HOMESTEADER: They never bothered a hair on his head. Those Shawnee knew that Johnny Appleseed cared for the woods and the land as much as they did. And that he was doing everything he could to help the land flourish and prosper. And that mattered more to them than what color skin he had or where he was born.

(LIGHTS OUT on HOMESTEADER and SON, who exit left. LIGHTS UP RIGHT as A SETTLER'S FAMILY—SETTLER, SET-TLER'S WIFE, SETTLER'S BOY, SETTLER'S GIRL—enters and sits down at the table behind and to the right of log; they greet JOHNNY; he walks over to their table, and they invite him to sit.)

SETTLER: Tell us the news of the world, Johnny! Haven't seen a news-paper in over a year. Are we still at war with Mexico?

SETTLER'S WIFE: Now, Caleb, let Mr. Appleseed catch his breath and set a spell. You can catch up on the world outside Indiana later—not that you really need to.

(JOHNNY pulls out items from his sack; boy and girl press close to him.)

JOHNNY APPLESEED: Look what I found along the way. For you, young lady, a few bits of calico to make your dolly a new dress. And for you, young sir, here's an Indian arrowhead I picked up near San-dusky. Must be a thousand years old.

BOY AND GIRL: Thanks, Mr. Appleseed!

JOHNNY APPLESEED: And for Ma and Pa—here's some seeds for a pear tree. A fellow gave 'em to me last month down along the Muskingum. And I've got some pages from a new book to read you tonight—an English writer named Dickens tells stories about common working folk.

SETTLER'S WIFE: Thank you so much, Mr. Appleseed. Now, won't you have supper with us?

JOHNNY APPLESEED: I will! But only if you're sure you have enough for the children.

SETTLER: We've got plenty, Johnny. Thanks to you, we had a good harvest this year—our best ever. Now, tell us about that terrible potato famine in Ireland…

(LIGHTS OUT ON SETTLER FAMILY; SPOTLIGHT UP RIGHT ON TEEN GIRL AND TEEN BOY.)

TEEN GIRL: After supper, Johnny read for awhile, and then he went to sleep next to the fireplace. He died in his sleep, at the age of seventy-two. He was buried in one of his beloved apple orchards.

TEEN BOY: Wow! So *that* was Johnny Appleseed? He was, like, way cool giving food to people and helping them grow food for themselves!

TEEN GIRL: Definitely. Because of people like him, the United States is the most productive agricultural nation on earth. We feed the world.

TEEN BOY: So, how come there's, like, people still starving in the world? And nature is still being destroyed with pollution and toxic chemicals?

TEEN GIRL: Oh. That's because of Willie Crabgrass.

TEEN BOY: Willie Crabgrass? Who's that?

TEEN GIRL: Willie Crabgrass was Johnny Appleseed's cousin. They didn't get along too well. People just naturally seemed to like Johnny, but nobody much wanted to have anything to do with Willie at all. It was a personality thing. Johnny spent his whole life being kind and friendly and helpful to everyone he met. But Willie, he was always rude and nasty, and he was really jealous of all the positive attention Johnny got for his good deeds.

TEEN BOY: Yeh, sounds like some people I know. Just can't stand to see somebody cool do their thing. *(runs comb through hair, preens)*

TEEN GIRL: *(frowns at him)* After both boys grew up, Johnny had found his life's work—sowing and planting, helping make the Earth a more bountiful place. But Willie, he went the other way. He sowed and planted, all right, but it was crabgrass and weeds. And discord.

(SPOTLIGHT OUT; LIGHTS UP CENTER STAGE on JOHNNY APPLESEED sowing seeds. At stage left, WILLIE CRABGRASS peeks from behind the curtain and watches Johnny for a few moments, as if spying on him. Then he swaggers foppishly to center and addresses JOHNNY.)

WILLIE CRABGRASS: Well if it isn't Mr. Sunshine and Buzzy Bees!

JOHNNY APPLESEED: Cousin Willie! How are you?

WILLIE CRABGRASS: Perfect as usual. I see you're still grubbing around in the soil.

JOHNNY APPLESEED: You bet. And I'm glad you came by, cousin. I sure could use some help with this new orchard.

WILLIE CRABGRASS: Help? Yes, I bet you could. You could use a visit to the noodle doctor. *(taps finger on his head)* You'd find that very helpful. When are you going to smarten up and get out of this game?

JOHNNY APPLESEED: Get out? Why, cousin, this is the biggest game on earth. In fact, it's what the earth is all about. Planting…growing…spreading the bounty of nature on every continent for everyone to share. Come join me, Willie; with two of us working together, we can double the harvest this year.

WILLIE CRABGRASS: Cousin, you're full of more sap than a maple tree. Why, you should join *me* and make a fortune taming this wilderness. I built ten new coal mines in West Virginia last week. Ripped up a few mountains that were in the way…but I made a fortune! *(laughs)*

JOHNNY APPLESEED: Willie, there's a difference between taming the wilderness and destroying it.

WILLIE CRABGRASS: You're right, cousin. The difference is that I'm rich, and you're walking around barefoot in the snow eating cornmush.

JOHNNY APPLESEED: You don't really believe what you're doing is good for this country.

WILLIE CRABGRASS: Don't I? Cousin, I am no hypocrite! I'll have you know that Willie Crabgrass is a man who stands by his beliefs! *(to audience)* Even if they are twisted and criminal. *(to JOHNNY)* Tell you what…let's make a small wager.

JOHNNY APPLESEED: A wager? I have nothing with which to gamble!

WILLIE CRABGRASS: Sure you do. You've got your reputation as a legend—Mr. Johnny Appleseed, the biggest seed-sower in America. I propose a contest: to decide which of us is truly the greatest planter. Starting today, we grow a country…*this* country, the United States of America. I plant it my way; you plant it yours. And when it's all planted from coast to coast, we'll see whose seeds have sprouted and come out on top.

JOHNNY APPLESEED: Sounds fair to me. Shake, cousin. *(offers his hand)*

WILLIE CRABGRASS: Why, certainly.

(WILLIE does a trick handshake—offering his hand, then jerking it away at the last minute and strolling off left, laughing. JOHNNY rolls up sleeves and begins sowing; WILLIE enters from left with torch and a Colt revolver. Both JOHNNY and WILLIE mime actions in ensuing dialogue, working faster and more feverishly.)

TEEN GIRL: *(o.s.)* The contest had begun. Johnny, of course, sowed farms and orchards; Willie laid down railroad track over the fields Johnny had just planted. Johnny encouraged tracts of preserves for delicate wildlife; Willie shot thousands of buffalo from passing trains. Johnny planted oaks that grew into mighty forests; Willie sent in lumbering crews that sliced the timber into sawdust—and then started forest fires to finish the job. Johnny nourished creeks and lakes and rivers, doing his best to keep them pure and fresh for future generations; Willie built huge factories and sprawling cities that threw their sewage and waste into every single artery of the country's water system. Finally, after more than a century, the two cousins met up and compared what they'd accomplished.

(WILLIE CRABGRASS stands at center stage, faces audience and spreads his arms out.)

WILLIE CRABGRASS: Look at this! It's amazing! It's almost the 21st century, and there is barely a blade of grass that hasn't been bought and sold twenty times over! And thanks to that fellow Ford, there's enough automobiles to cover the entire surface of the planet! And, when they run out of gas, we just dump 'em in the oceans! *(laughs)* Will you admit, cousin, that I am the greatest sower on earth?

(JOHNNY steps up beside him.)

JOHNNY APPLESEED: *(wearily)* You have labored very hard, cousin. Your efforts have made a lasting mark on the world. There are millions of Americans who have never tasted a fresh fruit or vegetable. Or enjoyed an unsullied mouthful of water or breath of unpolluted air.

WILLIE CRABGRASS: That's right! They get their food from little boxes…frozen, fossilized, stamped out of a steel mold in a factory by machines. And they actually buy water in plastic bottles! Can you *believe* it? *(laughs)*

JOHNNY APPLESEED: Even so, America still grows enough to feed a very hungry world.

WILLIE CRABGRASS: But machines have defeated your precious nature, cousin! Machines have *replaced* nature! Machines rule the world!

JOHNNY APPLESEED: In the right hands those machines have been used to heal diseases. To allow men to walk on the moon and sail through the sky to the front gates of the very heavens.

WILLIE CRABGRASS: Hah! The very heavens that are littered with tons of space trash. *(to audience)* Pssst! Anybody wanna buy a used Sputnik? Got a redhot vintage Skylab for peanuts!

JOHNNY APPLESEED: There are lots of people that think like you, Willie. But you will never win. Each thing in this world that is planted and grows has its own seed for creating another living thing. Apples, pears, oats, bananas, animals and people—this planet is still growing after millions and millions of years. And it never will stop as long as we continue to spin around the Sun. Because even this galaxy, Willie, is a seed; the seed for thousands upon thousands of other galaxies and solar systems throughout the universe. All of them growing, all of them bursting with blessed, beautiful bounty.

WILLIE CRABGRASS: So, you won't admit that I, Willie Crabgrass, am the greatest sower? The greatest planter? Well, I think you're a sore loser, cousin. Let's ask these people here who won the contest. Me? *(solicits audience applause)* Or him? *(Whatever the response, WILLIE is disgusted.)* Ah, you're all a bunch of saps! Cousin, I'll see you again in another century. We'll see then who this world belongs to: Johnny Appleseed…or Willie Crabgrass.

(WILLIE exits left; JOHNNY speaks to the audience.)

JOHNNY APPLESEED: Another century…can this precious earth of ours last that long? This world belongs to all of you sitting out there today. But you can't just sit and watch. You've got to take responsibility for making the world the way *you* want it to be. Willie's world…or mine. It's your choice. Here, I've got some extra seeds, if anybody wants to plant your own orchard. I'll meet you round back after the show. So long, friends. *(exits left)*

(SPOTLIGHT UP RIGHT ON TEEN GIRL AND TEEN BOY.)

TEEN BOY: That Willie Crabgrass is one scary dude. Like, wacko!

TEEN GIRL: No duh. Reminds me of a homeroom monitor I had in sixth grade.

TEEN BOY: Yeh. So, you wanna go to the Bongo Puppy Whistle concert Saturday night?

TEEN GIRL: Concert? The fate of the world is hanging in the balance, and the most important thing on your mind is a Bongo Puppy Whistle concert?

TEEN BOY: Well…yeh!

(TEEN GIRL jumps up in disgust.)

TEEN BOY: But maybe before we went to the concert, we could help pull some weeds in the community garden downtown.

TEEN GIRL: Or clean up some litter along the creek.

TEEN BOY: Yeh. It's more fun to be outdoors, anyway. *(rises)*

(TEEN GIRL puts her lunch trash in trash basket; TEEN BOY does likewise but retains an apple he holds in his hand.)

TEEN GIRL: *(moves right toward exit)* See you later.

TEEN BOY: I'll call you tomorrow.

TEEN GIRL: Okay. *(waves, exits)*

(TEEN BOY moves left toward exit, stops, holds out the apple toward audience.)

TEEN BOY: No doubt about it, that Johnny Appleseed *is* one cool dude. He not only made the world a healthier place…he just got me a date! *(exits)*

THE END

THE FLAMES OF HELL
(Les Flammes d'Enfer)

Many folk songs have very interesting stories about how they were created, sometimes in circumstances involving the spirit world. *Les Flammes d'Enfer* (*The Flames of Hell* in English) is a dance tune and song played by Cajun musicians in Louisiana. Cajun music is the folk music of the French-speaking people (originally called "Acadiens" and then "Cajuns") who immigrated to Louisiana from Canada in the late 1700s, settling mostly in the bayou country west of New Orleans. In the last few years Cajun music has become popular across the United States and throughout the world.

TIME: Mardi Gras Eve, 1954

PLACE: A lonely bayou in southwest Louisiana

CAST: Tee Emile   Robert Johnson
       Aldus Fontenot   Bix Beiderbecke
       Talent Agent   Jimmie Rodgers
       Angeline Peltier   Hank Williams, Sr.
       Rufus Duhon   Amédée Ardoin
       Aldus' Mother   4 Dancers/Neighbors (2 male, 2 female)

STAGE SET: a swampy landscape—a backdrop can be hung with several trees painted/hung with dark, heavy moss; a pirogue (rowboat) in center; to the left and a few feet upstage from the pirogue is a black curtain with two holes cut in it at waist height (this is an automobile, and "headlights" can be simulated by having clip lights shine through them from behind curtain)

PROPS: soup; bowl; sauce bottles; pirogue; oar; accordion; guitar; walking stick; cigar; contract

SPECIAL EFFECTS: sound: swamp noises (owls, frogs, lapping water against boat), crashing thunder, lightning crack, engine roar, jazzy 1920s' trumpet tootle, accordion sounds; visual: lighting flash, headlights, smoke

MUSIC: *Les Flammes d'Enfer; Dennis McGee's Two-Step*

COSTUMES: Tee Emile, Tante Louise, Aldus Fontenot, Angeline Peltier, Rufus Duhon and the Dancers/Neighbors dress in 1950s' rural styles; Mr. Talent Agent Man dresses in a white suit with black bow tie, white fedora and two-tone leather shoes; Robert Johnson and Bix Beiderbecke wear dark dress suits; Jimmie Rodgers wears his "Singing Brakeman" outfit; Hank Williams, Sr. wears a Western stetson hat and suit; Amédée Ardoin is dressed in overalls

Stage Plan -- *The Flames of Hell*

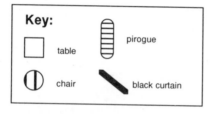

(MUSIC FADES IN: "Les Flammes d'Enfer," a lonesome Cajun tune in 4/4 meter, is played on accordion; LIGHTS UP on a man, TEE EMILE, sitting at a table stage right, carefully stirring a soup bowl and sprinkling seasonings into it from various sauce bottles.)

TEE EMILE: *(sings along as music fades)*…"oh little aunt, pray for me, I'm condemned to the flames of hell…pray for me, save my soul, save my soul from the flames of hell"…And them are touts les mots to *"Les Flammes d'Enfer,"* ou en Americain, "The Flames of Hell." Don't that pretty? You what? You never hear that tune before? Well, there you got it now, cher, straight from the gator's mouth, straight from Tee Emile. Story! Ah, mais oui! There is always a story behind the making of every Cajun tune, and the story behind that one is true as I'm sitting here right now. Here, let me fix you up another pile of that good gumbo, s'il vous plait. Mmm-mmm, I lovvvvvve them hot pepper—le bon temps est apres me tuer! The good times are killing me!

(SOUND: accordion chord in and out several times.)

TEE EMILE: *(takes a big bite of gumbo)* So you want to hear stories about the bayou? Well now, this one story was way many year ago, back about nineteen and fifty-three or maybe four, when I myself was in my courting days. There was a young boy name of Aldus Fontenot, who live with his family, his mother and father, his nonc et tante, his gramere et grapere and a whole mess of younger brothers and sisters, not far from here in St. Mary Parish along the Bayou Teche, way back in the deep, deep, deep swamp past Verdunville and Bayou Vista, just above Sweet Bay Lake nearly to where the Atchafalaya run itself into the Gulf down by Point Dent de Sorciere—the Witch's Tooth...now that is a story for another time in itself...Like the rest of their kind, these Fontenot were simple people, living off the bayou for generation upon generation, always ready to lend un coupe de main—a helping hand—to a neighbor or passing traveler.

(ALDUS FONTENOT enters from left, lowers himself into the pirogue at center stage, picks up an oar and begins paddling lightly.)

TEE EMILE: One dark winter night, the night before Mardi Gras, young Aldus Fontenot sat in his nonc Maurice's pirogue in a gloomy cypress grove on the banks of the bayou. Aldus was sixteen year old, handsome like his pere and a good fisherman, already a man in many ways and just getting to be a man in others. And like so many young men then and now, he wanted more than anything to go out from his small, comfortable boyhood home and make his mark upon the big world outside St. Mary Parish...to be recognized and applauded and adored by millions of people he had never seen...but wished with all his heart could see him and love him like the hero he felt himself to be.

(ALDUS stops rowing, settles back and stretches his arms; he picks up an accordion from the bottom of the boat and runs his fingers gingerly—but soundlessly—over the buttons.)

TEE EMILE: At this moment, pourtant, Aldus was tres, tres miserable. For the last five hour he had sat in the pirogue with his father's accordion trying with all his might to master a simple two-step.

(ALDUS tries to play the accordion; SOUND: badly off-key accordion stumbling through a tune.)

TEE EMILE: He say—

ALDUS: You no-good piece of dumb crazy tuneless junk!

(SOUND: accordion screech.)

ALDUS: Mocking me with your squealy clanks!

(SOUND: accordion screech.)

ALDUS: Aiiiieeeee! What I'm gonna did with you?

(He puts accordion down in front of him, and leans on the front of the boat, head in hands.)

TEE EMILE: Skilled as he was in the ways of the bayou, Aldus was not likely to become a rich man from his musical talent, mais non. To be sure, when he start to play the accordion, it was with as much grace as a yellowfoot chicken running through the barnyard with its wings on fire. Écoute! He could make a sweet yam turn sour and a jug of white-mule moonshine go flat as rainwater with one screaming honk of that thing! What made Aldus two, even three time more frustrated this night, was he was trying to learn this tune to play at the big fais-do-do set for tomorrow at the home of Bluebell Sonnier.

(MUSIC UP: Cajun music—"Dennis McGee's Two-Step"—on fiddle, accordion, guitar and triangle. FOUR DANCERS—two male, two female—enter from stage left and cross to center next to ALDUS; they laugh and cavort with each other, one carrying a jug, another a picnic basket. MUSIC FADES UNDER.)

TEE EMILE: Oh, it would be a big, big Mardi Gras party—the biggest in the parish! People from all cross the townland would come and dance all the night till break of dawn!

(ANGELINE PELTIER enters, shyly, from stage right, slowly crossing to center near the dancers.)

TEE EMILE: And so too, at this fais-do-do, and dancing to be sure, would be Angeline Peltier, a shy but tres populaire jeune fille from Point Chevreuil…about fifteen year old and oh, oh, so pretty!

(ALDUS sits up straight in pirogue and tries to catch ANGELINE'S eye.)

TEE EMILE: At Armille Toucet's big barn raising but two week before, Aldus danced and held hands with her, just long enough to have her set his silly head to spin and his foolish heart to pine with hopeless young love. She be so pretty he can't stood it!

ALDUS: Aiiiieeeee! *(reaches out to her, but she can't hear him)*

(RUFUS DUHON, a guitar slung over his shoulder, enters from stage left; he postures in front of ANGELINE, who pretends not to notice him but then becomes intrigued.)

TEE EMILE: But it seem the young mademoiselle had took much more of a shine to one Rufus Duhon, a guitar strummer with Popeye Broussard's Jeanerette Playboys.

(ANGELINE dances as if with a partner, but looks over her shoulder toward RUFUS, who casts her sly glances.)

TEE EMILE: Aldus could not help to notice that even when she danced with him, Aldus—when they even danced close—her beautiful green eyes were all on a wander around the room to seek Duhon and his strummy guitar. Aldus say:

ALDUS: If I could play this old accordion much more better, ma belle Angeline would pay attention to *me* and not Rufus Duhon. Why, I believe I would do just about *anything* to be the best accordion player in the world! I believe to my soul I would, indeed!

(MUSIC FADES OUT DURING LAST LINE; LIGHTS DIM TO THREE-QUARTER; ANGELINE, RUFUS and DANCERS exit left; SOUND: swamp noises—owls, frogs, lapping water, etc.)

TEE EMILE: So Aldus sit in the pirogue, all alone in the dark, dark swamp, brooding so mournful upon his beloved…

(SPOTLIGHT ON ALDUS; SOUND: CRASHING THUNDER.)

TEE EMILE: When all of a sudden, there come a blaze of bright white light and the sound of roaring thunder crashing through the cypress right on top of him.

(SOUND: LIGHTNING CRACK; ALDUS leaps out of boat, left; headlights flash at him from behind hanging black curtain.)

TEE EMILE: Up he jump, right out of his pirogue onto the bank where he come face to face with a big black Cadillac car standing smack in front of him not twenty feet away, its motor running like a pack of quartermile bobtails on race day at St. Martinville fair.

(SOUND: RACING CAR ENGINE.)

ALDUS: Who dat? Who dat dere in dat big black Cadillac?

TEE EMILE: And, of course, Aldus is all at wondering just a little at how a Cadillac Coupe de Ville had got itself all the way into this part of the bayou—but he see no harm in being friendly.

ALDUS: Hey, you looking for crawfish? Best place to catch some be up around the bend ahead! Never heard of anybody go fishing in a Cadillac.

(SOUND: ENGINE STOPS; CAR DOOR OPENS: RED SPOT-LIGHT ON CURTAIN.)

TEE EMILE: The motor cut out and the driver door, it slowly—verrrrrry slowly—open. Through the mist that surround the Cadillac, Aldus could see a tall, thin man—tall and thin like a pitchfork with leather shoes.

(LIGHTS UP FULL as TALENT AGENT steps out from behind curtain, confident and self-assured, twirlng a bright red walking stick.)

TEE EMILE: The man begin to walk toward Aldus, and as he come closer, Aldus see that the man is all dress up like some state politician and sporting by his side a fancy walking stick that glow bright red in the darkness, almost like it was on fire. And then the man stop walking, pulls out a paper from his jacket and start to talk:

TALENT AGENT: *(an intensely New York/Brooklyn accent)* Are youse Aldus Fontenot of Cahcahoula Ridge, Parish of St. Mary, State of Louisiana, U.S. of A.? *(points stick at ALDUS' chest)*

ALDUS: *(takes a step back)* That what they call me.

TEE EMILE: Say Aldus back to the man, just a 'tee bit fidgety at the way the fellow's words seem to jump right out the end of that bright red stick and just hang in the air like big shiny red fingers. But he reply, calmly:

ALDUS: What they call you?

TALENT AGENT: *(circles around ALDUS)* Junior, ya can call me your meal ticket to Easy Street on the Gravy Train Express! My name's not important—don't trifle yourself with menials, son—while you're about to make a decision guaranteed to change your life from now till forever. *(backs up ALDUS against the pirogue)*

ALDUS: Heyyyyy. . .

TALENT AGENT: All ya need to know, kid, is that I represent—in person—the largest personal management agency in the world. That's Cabal, Ruse and Knavery, Unlimited, with offices in every country you can think of, and some ya can't cause they ain't been invented yet, but we'll be there when they are, ya can bet your last chunka crawfish on that, sonny.

ALDUS: What you want with me, monsieur? I have no, no talent.

TALENT AGENT: I'll ask the questions. Now, I hear ya wanna be famous all over the world, right?

ALDUS: Oui, monsieur.

TALENT AGENT: And rich?

ALDUS: Mais, oui!

TALENT AGENT: Ya wanna have women go crazy for you? Runnin' after you wherever you go? For the rest of your natural life…and beyond?

ALDUS: Mais, oui, monsieur! Mais oui! What I got to did to be this kind of famous?

TALENT AGENT: Not so fast, junior. First, lemme tell ya about some of our clients.

(MUSIC: blues chords played on twangy bottleneck guitar; ROBERT JOHNSON enters from right, holding a guitar; he strolls to ALDUS and shakes his hand, then stands behind TALENT AGENT.)

TALENT AGENT: Ever hear of Robert Johnson, the sensational Mississippi Delta blues guitarist?

ALDUS: But of course. My cousin Lionel have all his records.

TALENT AGENT: Well, I gave him his start.

ALDUS: Mais, non!

TALENT AGENT: Couldn't play a lick when he signed up with us, not a lick. Then—pizzamarooni!—overnight every record company in America was fightin' over him tooth an' nail. Just like that.

TEE EMILE: His walking stick did a double flip over his head and hung by his side about two feet off the ground, like it was keeping watch on Aldus.

TALENT AGENT: And that jazz trumpet tooter from the Midwest, Bix Beiderbecke.

(SOUND: jazzy 1920s' trumpet tootle; BIX BEIDERBECKE enters from left, holding a trumpet; he strolls to center, tips his trumpet, then stands behind TALENT AGENT with ROBERT JOHNSON.)

TALENT AGENT: You heard of him, too, I s'pose? Couldn't hit a high C before we took him on. And Jimmie Rodgers, the Singing Brakeman character in the choo-choo cap?

(SOUND: a whooping, hillybilly-style yodel. JIMMIE RODGERS enters from right; he strolls to center, tips his cap, then stands behind TALENT AGENT with others.)

TALENT AGENT: Sold millions of records! Millions! Made a couple movies, too, after he signed with our firm. And the other hillbilly guy, big star, from Alabama, what was his name, lessee, it temporarily deludes me—

ALDUS: *(holds hand over his heart)* Do you speak of Mister Hank Williams?

(SOUND: first two bars of "Hey, Good Lookin'" played on fiddle; HANK WILLIAMS, SR. enters from left; he strolls to center, gives ALDUS a big wave, then stands behind TALENT AGENT with others.)

TALENT AGENT: One an' the same. Signed him myself.

ALDUS: You know all these fabulous musicians?

TALENT AGENT: Know 'em? Hah! Junior, they got it all from me. Matter a fact, there was a yegg a few years back from around these parts. Squeezebox player like yourself; skinny little guy named, named, uh, lessee, got it right here in the book…oh yeh—Amy Dee Ardawon.

(SOUND: D chord on accordion squeezed in and out; AMÉDÉE ARDOIN enters from left, holding an accordion; he strolls to center, bows to ALDUS, then stands behind TALENT AGENT with others.)

TEE EMILE: When he hear this name, Aldus was beside himself with all kind of crazy pleasure.

ALDUS: Amédée Ardoin? The Amédée Ardoin from Basile? Monsieur talent agent, Amédée Ardoin, he is my hero, the greatest Cajun accordion player of all time!

TALENT AGENT: One an' the same, kid, one an' the same. Say, how'd you like to be able to play just like him? Tonight?

ALDUS: Like him! I would give anything to play like the great Amédée Ardoin! But surely you joke with me, monsieur. How can I, Aldus Fontenot, ever—

TALENT AGENT: Easy kid. Toss me that squeezola.

TEE EMILE: And the accordion jump right out of Aldus' hands into the long skinny arms of the talent agent.

(ALDUS tosses accordion to TALENT AGENT.)

TALENT AGENT: Come to papa!

TEE EMILE: And then the man place his hands on either side of the bellows, just like this here…and he pump them three time…very hard…and the accordion she give a loud, low moan…

(SOUND: tremolo lowest note on accordion.)

TEE EMILE: A moan like the very life done got squeeze out of her…and left this world altogether.

(TALENT AGENT tosses accordion to ALDUS.)

TALENT AGENT: Now try that tune you were noodlin' with awhile ago…

TEE EMILE: Say the talent agent, and the accordion leap back into Aldus' hands. Well now, cher—Aldus run his fingers over the buttons and—c'est miraculeux!

(SOUND: quick accordion scale, then "The Flames of Hell" played double-time; LIGHTS FLASH AND STROBE; JOHNSON, BEIDERBECKE, RODGERS, WILLIAMS and ARDOIN clap and shout.)

TEE EMILE: All of a sudden, he can play the tune sans erreur, note for each perfect note flying from his fingers through the black night air, notes of ruby red and notes of golden yellow and notes of sky blue and royal purple and shining silver and emerald green, every color note in the whole wide world jumping and leaping and dancing and whirling out of his accordeon through the bayou mist, spelling words he have never seen in ancient tongues he have never heard, making shapes of pyramids and moons and dragons that talk and call his name over and over and over in the voice of his beloved Angeline. . .

(SOUND: chorus calling "Aldus," then a woman's voice calling, ending in a deep sighing.)

WOMAN: *(o.s.)* Aldus…Aldus…oh, Aldus, mon ami…mon amour

(MUSIC STOPS; LIGHTS STOP FLASHING, RETURN UP FULL.)

TEE EMILE: And Aldus play every Cajun tune he ever want to play—

(MUSIC: "Dennis McGee's Two-Step" played by accordion.)

TEE EMILE:—the banaille…the fuseille…the valse Julien…quadrilles …mazurkas…polkas…reels…two-steps…le tee Moreau… the shoo-fly…la jolie blon'…the shimmy…old baisse-bas, and even a few fancy coudinnes—just because he could!

ALDUS: Aiiiieeeee!

(He dances, prances, gets on bended knee, pirouettes, plays accordion over his head, behind his back, pogoing—completely overwhelmed with the music.)

TEE EMILE: Hour after hour after wonderful hour he played and played and played…

(MUSIC STOPS.)

TEE EMILE: Till finally, the music stop leaping out of his accordion, and Aldus fell down all out of breath in front of the talent agent leaning on his walking stick and chewing on a big green cigar.

ALDUS: *(huffing, breathless)* Ai-ai-aieeeeuh! Hoo-hah! Yowww…

TALENT AGENT: See, kid, I knew ya had it in ya. Now let's make this all nice an' legal.

TEE EMILE: And from the top of his walking stick, the talent agent man pull out a looonnng, looonnng piece of paper, which he put right in front of Aldus.

TALENT AGENT: Just a standard management contract, sonny. Standard, absolutely standard.

ALDUS: *(up on his feet)* What do it say, this contract?

TALENT AGENT: Simply a formality…gives the agency exclusive sovereignty and universal permanent title to your complete and total personage and entity, physical and supra-physical, not withstanding any accrued performance credits, publishing or recording royalties and legitimate and/or non-legitimate offspring concurrent with and/or from this date forward in the exercise of the purchaser's sole prerogative to enjoy and reap all benefits and rewards herewith and thereof, deriving from the purchasee and his/her assigns now until forever—did I mention this was really *forever?*—including this life and those hereafter…thereby, be it expressly understood to comprise all rights and permissions to which as purchaser the undersigned be fully and duly and therein entitled. Sign here, kid, right on the dotted line.

TEE EMILE: Aldus push away the pen floating in front of his eyes.

ALDUS: Une minute, monsieur. Them is a very lot of words. Perhaps I better stop and look on that.

TALENT AGENT: *(snatches paper away)* Huh? Nah, don't trouble yourself with trivials, kid. Everybody signs this contract just the way it is. Johnson, Beiderbecke, Rodgers, Williams, Ardoin…all your heroes, kid…all your heroes.

TEE EMILE: The names danced in front of Aldus' eyes, swirled about his head, tickled his chin, whispered in his ears…

(SOUND: accordion, fiddle, guitar, trumpet wails crescendo, then under; ALDUS paces, shakes his head, rubs his eyes as the TALENT AGENT taps his feet impatiently, looks at watch, chews cigar.)

TEE EMILE:…until Aldus start to realize something about these great musicians. He realize all and every one of these great musical heroes—these heroes loved by millions—have died miserable and alone. Each and every one, all.

(MUSIC FADES, STOPS; ALDUS turns to TALENT AGENT.)

ALDUS: This Robert Johnson…could this be the Robert Johnson who got poison to death by his jealous girlfriend?

(ROBERT JOHNSON walks slowly to center, lowers his head and exits right.)

TALENT AGENT: Whazzat, kid? You say somethin'?

ALDUS: And this Monsieur Beiderbecke, did he not die of drinking very bad moonshine?

(BIX BEIDERBECKE walks slowly to center, shrugs his shoulders and exits left.)

TALENT AGENT: Wellllll. . .

ALDUS: And Jimmie Rodgers, he pass away very young of tuberculosis, je crois. And Mister Hank Williams…why, he die all alone, freezing to death, in the back seat of his car.

(RODGERS and WILLIAMS walk slowly to center, bow to ALDUS, exit right.)

TALENT AGENT: Listen, Pierre, we're startin' to drift. I'm offerin' you the deal of a lifetime—several lifetimes, in fact. Now, let's you and me just sign this little contract here—

ALDUS: And Amédée Ardoin, I know he die just thirteen year ago…in the Pineville House for the Insane.

(ARDOIN shuffles to center, turns around twice, shuffles off left, letting the air out of his accordion.)

TALENT AGENT: Kid, don't worry, nonna that's gonna happen to you, kid. I'll take care of everything, trust me.

(ALDUS says nothing; the TALENT AGENT pushes the contract in his face.)

TALENT AGENT: Look, I don't got all night to be soakin' my knickers shootin' the swamp breeze. Okay, I'm wise—you're hoistin' a torch for that stuckup Angeline toots. C'mon, forget about these local sows and sign here. You're gonna be big-time now! You'll get all the babes you'll ever want. More than you'll ever want!

TEE EMILE: Well now, this kind of disreputatious talk about his favorite girl, and the girls of St. Mary Parish, start to make Aldus plenty mad.

ALDUS: *(pushes TALENT AGENT away)* Attend, monsieur! Attend, s'il vous plait! I am a Fontenot, and a Fontenot man can gain the hand of any woman he desire.

TALENT AGENT: That a fact? Bunch of regular Romeos, eh?

ALDUS: A Fontenot man need no tricks. No voodoo spell. No magic potions. And no assistance from un gigolo...un mackerel...un satyre!

TALENT AGENT: *(straightens his bow tie, dusts off his sleeves)* Suit yourself, junior.

(The TALENT AGENT snaps his fingers and gives a sharp whistle; LIGHTS FLASH AND GO DARK FOR THREE SECONDS; the Cadillac headlights blaze up, motor races; LIGHTS RETURN TO FULL.)

TALENT AGENT: So tell me which way's the road to Memphis? Got an appointment with a hillbilly cat from Tupelo, some crazy-legs guitar picker named Melvis...Pelvis...Schmelvis-something—I dunno... all these Confederate names slay the heck outa me.

TEE EMILE: Aldus point to the north and—flash!

(SOUND: THUNDER CRASH, LIGHTNING CRACK, ENGINE ROAR; TALENT AGENT steps behind curtain, exits.)

TEE EMILE: The Cadillac and the talent agent man with the bright red walking stick were gone—just in the instant you blink your eye, cher! Not a trace of the man or his car but a thin puff of black, black smoke twisting slowly through the live oak trees and cypress.

(SOUND: THUNDER, LIGHTNING, ENGINE NOISE FADE.)

ALDUS: Hooowheeee!

TEE EMILE: Say Aldus, rubbing first one eye then another, then both at the same time to make sure this is not some kind of dream, and he is not really in his own bed at home.

ALDUS: Don't that beat all! Aiiiieeeee! No more squirrel jambalaya and gaspergou gumbo pour moi! Quelle chance...there is the sun about ready to rise itself. I best get back in my pirogue and go on to home. Come on, you squeezey fellow you…

(He picks up the accordion from the ground.)

ALDUS: But what is this? *(examines accordion with awe)*

TEE EMILE: And now in the bright light of the waking dawn, when Aldus pick up his accordion, what do you think—but there were two big burn marks on either side of the bellows…burn marks like big flames…or huge big burning hands—right where that talent agent man had squeezed it.

ALDUS: Mon dieu de tout le monde!

(ALDUS gets into pirogue and rows quickly, looking around and over his shoulder nervously.)

TEE EMILE: Each finger of each hand burned into the accordion was in the shape of an animal claw…not an alligator or grizzly or puma, cher, but something almost human…yet too much more horrible to ever imagine meeting by your lonesome…in the middle of the dark bayou.

(THE FOUR DANCERS/NEIGHBORS, ANGELINE and ALDUS' MOTHER enter from right and congregate around table, murmuring to each other as ALDUS steps out of pirogue and puts the accordion on the table.)

TEE EMILE: When Aldus got back to his home and show his accordion to his family and neighbors, they all say:

ALDUS' MOTHER: These, my son, these are the flames of hell. That talent agent man was the devil, and these be his mark, the mark he was hoping to put upon your eternal soul.

(SOUND: THUNDER CRASHING; everyone cowers, then hugs and congratulates ALDUS.)

TEE EMILE: And ever since that day, the tune that Aldus was playing that night in the bayou is known as *"Les Flammes d'Enfer"*—*"The Flames of Hell."*

(MUSIC: "Les Flammes d'Enfer," played by accordion, slow and lonesome under dialogue; the NEIGHBORS and ALDUS' MOTHER drift off to exits; ALDUS and ANGELINE clasp hands and dance to music, eyes only for each other.)

TEE EMILE: Now, that is the truth, cher, and I am most happy to have tell it to you *exactly* the way it happen. No, I do not know what became of that particular accordion…but I can tell you for a fact that later that same year, Aldus Fontenot made Angeline Peltier his wife, and they lived happy as can be over by Lake de Cade in Terrebonne Parish…until Aldus went to the Vietnam and got killed in nineteen and sixty-four or was it sixty-five? But his family—Madame Angeline, two strong sons and two lovely, lovely daughters—they all live over in Terrebonne still, some by Dulac and Boudreaux, one by Lake Theriot and another near Houma the last I hear. Et tous les enfants et grandkids, aussi, they all play the good Cajun music on fiddle and accordion and mouth organ…and they all play *"Les Flammes d'Enfer"*…the way Aldus Fontenot learned it that Mardi Gras Eve in the bayou.

(LIGHTS OUT; MUSIC UP UNTIL END OF TUNE.)

THE END

The Flames of Hell (Les Flammes d'Enfer)

(traditional, arranged by L.E. McCullough)

Oh, 'tite tante pri- ez pour moi

Je suis con- damné pour les flammes d'en- fer

Pri- ez pour moi sau- vez mon âme

sau- vez mon âme pour les flammes d'en- fer

English Words: Oh little aunt, pray for me, I'm condemned to the flames of hell
Pray for me, save my soul, save my soul from the flames of hell

Dennis McGee's Two-Step

(traditional, arranged by L.E. McCullough)

ABE LINCOLN FOR THE DEFENSE

Abe Lincoln for the Defense is based upon a stirring criminal trial in which Abraham Lincoln successfully defended the son of an old friend against murder charges. Lincoln began studying law in 1831 while living in the village of New Salem, Illinois, where he worked as local postmaster and deputy county surveyor. He was licensed as an attorney in 1836 and traveled the state as a "circuit-riding lawyer" known for his honesty, shrewdness and unique rapport with juries. Often he declined to accept a fee from a poor client and, in many instances, withdrew from cases upon discovering his client's cause was unjust. By 1858, when this play takes place, he was one of the leading attorneys in Illinois and the newly-nominated Republican candidate for the United States Senate—a campaign that would lead directly to his running for President two years later.

TIME: May, 1858

PLACE: Cass County Circuit Court, Beardstown, Illinois

CAST:
Beauford Q. Swap	Reporter
Abe Lincoln (adult)	Duff Armstrong
Abe Lincoln (child)	Mrs. Armstrong
Dr. Blake	Hugh Fullerton
Judge Harper	Charles Allen
Nelson Watkins	Bailiff
Nancy Lincoln	Nathan Chandler
Josiah Crawford	Old Soldier
Jury Foreman	5 Jury Members

STAGE SET: courtroom interior with 19 chairs and 3 tables; courthouse exterior with a hand-painted sign reading *Swap's Portable Emporium—Beardstown, Ill.*

PROPS: Swap's peddler bag; Reporter's notebook and pencil; 2 slingshots; handcuffs; Mrs. Armstrong's letter; Mrs. Armstrong's handkerchief; judge's gavel; Bible; almanac; Old Soldier's walking stick; Old Soldier's knapsack; Young Abe Lincoln's fishing pole; string of fish; Lincoln's pocket watch

COSTUMES: characters dress in mid-19th-century clothes with appropriate class and occupational distinctions: Hugh Fullerton, Judge, Dr. Blake and Reporter more formal than the Jury Members, spectators and witnesses and Beauford Q. Swap, who might dress somewhat more flamboyantly; Old Soldier wears an old military uniform; Abe Lincoln as an adult wears stovepipe hat, dark frock coat too long at the sleeves, dark trousers too short at the ankles, white shirt buttoned at neck without tie, unpolished black or brown knee boots—he is also clean-shaven

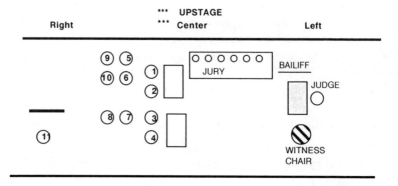

Stage Plan -- *Abe Lincoln for the Defense*

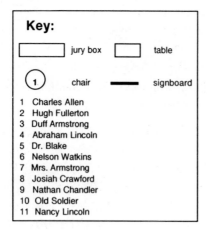

(LIGHTS UP. At stage right BEAUFORD Q. SWAP stands outside the courtroom hawking souvenirs in front of a painted signboard that reads "Swap's Portable Emporium—Beardstown, Ill."; lying at his feet is a canvas bag from which he pulls items to display aloft. He looks at the audience:)

SWAP: Step right up, ladies and gentlemen! Step right up and get your genu-wine souvenirs from the trial of the century!

(A NEWSPAPER REPORTER enters from right and strolls up to SWAP; SWAP hails him and holds up a slingshot.)

SWAP: Good day, friend, good day! Have you seen this bonafide facsimile of the hideous weapon Duff Armstrong used to kill Farmer Metzker? Only cost you one plugged nickel, three for a dime!

REPORTER: My good sir! Aren't you a bit hasty? The jury hasn't even heard the defense yet.

SWAP: Details, details! Jury's already made up their minds, and the gallows is half-finished over yonder! Say, you're not a family member, are you?

REPORTER: Hardly. I'm a reporter, from the *Muscatine Bugle-Thunderbolt*. That's in Iowa.

SWAP: All the way from I-o-way! I'll be switched! *(offers hand)* Beauford Q. Swap is my name, the Q stands for Quincy as in John Quincy Adams, a fellow son of New England's intrepid soil. I'm an honest peddler by trade, and I can give you the straight skinny on anything you need to know.

REPORTER: *(shakes SWAP'S hand)* Much obliged, Mr. Swap. *(takes out notebook and pencil)* What is your interpretation of the facts in the case?

(As SWAP and the REPORTER talk, various characters file into the courtroom interior from stage left and take their seats: state's attorney HUGH FULLERTON; witnesses DR. BLAKE, NELSON WATKINS and CHARLES ALLEN; spectators NATHAN CHANDLER, OLD SOLDIER and JOSIAH CRAWFORD; 5 JURY MEMBERS and JURY FOREMAN; BAILIFF leading a handcuffed DUFF ARMSTRONG, who stands and hangs his head in shame.)

SWAP: Here it is in a nutshell. Last August, there was a big camp meeting out in Mason County.

REPORTER: I attended a camp meeting once. It certified my belief that man was invented because God was disappointed in the monkey.

SWAP: Then you know how those affairs play out. After hearing about the Holy Spirit all day, come nighttime, folks want to get a little of the liquid spirit inside 'em.

REPORTER: Indeed. Man is the only animal that blushes—or needs to.

SWAP: Anyway, must've been close to midnight, when a stupendous confrontation broke out among the lads gathered round the sutler's wagon. Oh, whiskey was the cause of it, sure enough, and right smack dab in the center of the swinging was old Farmer Metzker and two young fellows, Jim Norris and Duff Armstrong. Now, everybody knows Metzker was about the nastiest bully in the Sangamon Valley and deserved a good hiding, but a witness says before it broke up, Norris hit the farmer in the back of the head with a wagon yoke and Armstrong whopped him in the eye with a slingshot. Next day, less than a mile away, they found Metzker fallen off his horse. He wasn't drunk no more, just dead.

REPORTER: I see. And the jury in Mason County has already found Jim Norris guilty?

SWAP: Guilty of manslaughter and ten years in the penitentiary.

REPORTER: Why didn't they try the other fellow, Armstrong, at the same time?

SWAP: Cause he got himself a smart lawyer, that's why. Couldn't get bail, but he got a change of venue to here in Beardstown.

(MRS. ARMSTRONG enters from left, walking slowly and unsteadily, handkerchief in her hand, hesitating at center stage.)

REPORTER: Who is the attorney for the defense?

SWAP: A curious sort of fellow by the name of—say, there's the boy's mother now!

REPORTER: *(approaches her)* Mrs. Armstrong! Mrs. Armstrong! I'm a reporter for the *Muscatine Bugle-Thunderbolt*, and I'd like to ask a few questions, if I may.

MRS. ARMSTRONG: *(distractedly)* Questions?

REPORTER: Yes. First of all, who have you hired to represent your son?

MRS. ARMSTRONG: *(pulls letter from her dress pocket and reads)* "My Dear Mrs. Armstrong: I have just heard of your affliction, and I am anxious that Duff be given a fair trial. Appreciation for the long-standing kindness your family has shown toward me prompts this offer of my humble services gratuitously in his behalf. Yours truly, Abraham Lincoln."

(She turns away and enters courtroom; REPORTER chuckles, addresses SWAP.)

REPORTER: Abraham Lincoln! Why, he's in the middle of a campaign for the United States Senate. He couldn't possibly have time to bother with a trifling local case—and ask no fee, to boot!

(MRS. ARMSTRONG stops, turns.)

MRS. ARMSTRONG: Young man, Abe Lincoln will never be too big nor too busy to help poor folks when they need him—even if he were the President of the United States. And you can print *that* in your newspaper!

(She enters courtroom; REPORTER writes down her remarks. JUDGE HARPER enters from left and takes his seat. SWAP pulls REPORTER to doorway.)

SWAP: There's Judge Harper. Old "Hanging Harper," they call him, cause of his predilection toward awarding a necktie party in capital cases. Come on, let's take a peek.

(SWAP and REPORTER enter courtoom, stand in back.)

JUDGE HARPER: *(strikes gavel)* Cass County Circuit Court is now in session, State versus Armstrong. *(looks around courtroom)* Where is the attorney for the defense? Mr. Lincoln! Mr. Abraham Lincoln!

MR. FULLERTON: *(snidely)* Probably splitting rails with his trusty harmonica.

(JURY MEMBERS, DR. BLAKE, NELSON WATKINS, CHARLES ALLEN and BAILIFF laugh; JUDGE HARPER Strikes gavel.)

JUDGE HARPER: Order in the court! I say, order in the court!

(Courtroom quiets as ABRAHAM LINCOLN enters nonchalantly from left, leisurely doffing his stovepipe hat, straightening his jacket, running his fingers through his hair.)

MR. LINCOLN: My apologies, your honor. Coming in on the train from Springfield this morning, I was accosted by a stranger who said, "Excuse me, sir, but I have an article in my possession that rightfully belongs to you." "How is that?" I replied. Whereupon the stranger produced a jackknife and pressed it into my palm, saying, "This knife was given to me some years ago with the injunction that I was to keep it until I met a man uglier than myself. Allow me now to say, sir, that I think you are fairly entitled to it."

(SPECTATORS laugh; JUDGE HARPER scowls.)

JUDGE HARPER: Mr. Lincoln, the floor is yours.

MR. LINCOLN: First off, I would like to introduce my client, Duff Armstrong. Duff, would you please stand and greet the folks?

(DUFF ARMSTRONG stands sheepishly; he smiles and nods, then sits.)

MR. LINCOLN: Thank you, son. I have known Duff since he was a baby. I count his mother and late father as among my closest friends. And it is to defend the honor of the Armstrong family, as well as the innocence of my client, that I stand before you today. Now, I would like to cross-examine Dr. Henry Blake.

(DR. BLAKE goes to the witness box; BAILIFF presents Bible for swearing in.)

BAILIFF: Do you solemnly swear to tell the truth and nothing but the truth, so help you God?

DR. BLAKE: I do.

MR. LINCOLN: Dr. Blake, I have read your notes detailing the nature of the deceased's wounds. They are extremely thorough and credit your reputation as a forensic expert of the first rank.

DR. BLAKE: Thank you, sir.

MR. LINCOLN: You are positive, beyond any question of doubt, that James Metzker died of a brain concussion due to the fractures you have described?

DR. BLAKE: I am.

MR. LINCOLN: Can you then state definitely whether these fractures were caused by blows of a club or a slingshot...or from a fall from a horse?

DR. BLAKE: Welllll....

MR. FULLERTON: *(rises)* I object! You honor, the defense is leading the witness!

JUDGE HARPER: Mr. Lincoln?

MR. LINCOLN: Your honor, I am not asking Dr. Blake for an opinion as to what specifically killed Mr. Metzger. I am asking only if it is within the power of medical science to provide such information.

JUDGE HARPER: Objection overruled. Witness, answer the question.

DR. BLAKE: Nosir, I cannot state *definitely* the cause of the fractures. A man as drunk as he was said to be might of died from anything hitting his skull.

MR. LINCOLN: Thank you, Doctor. That is all.

MR. FULLERTON: *(rises)* State calls Charles Allen.

(DR. BLAKE steps down and resumes his seat; as CHARLES ALLEN shuffles to the stand and is sworn in by BAILIFF, SWAP addresses the REPORTER.)

SWAP: That Allen is a squirrelly sort, ain't he? Won't even look a man in the eye.

REPORTER: Who is he?

SWAP: A weasel-nosed gambling buddy of old Metzker. It was his testimony got Jim Norris convicted.

MR. FULLERTON: Mr. Allen, please tell the court where you were the night of August twenty-ninth last.

ALLEN: I was at Virgin Grove in Mason County. Brother Willard had a big camp meetin' goin' on. Oh, there was some doin's that night!

MR. FULLERTON: And what were *you* doing at that meeting?

ALLEN: Er...nothin' much, I reckon.

(SPECTATORS, JURY laugh; JUDGE HARPER slaps gavel and court quiets.)

JUDGE HARPER: Witness, answer the question.

ALLEN: I was at the sutler's wagon. Playin' some poker...dancin' a little...*(chuckles)* drinkin' liquor mostly, I reckon.

MR. FULLERTON: I see. Now that we have you correctly located, I want you to tell the court what you saw while at the sutler's wagon.

ALLEN: I seen that feller Armstrong and his friend Norris standin' at the bar, wettin' their whistle with a dram of Kentucky's finest. Farmer Metzker, he come up behind 'em and he was plenty snozzled, staggerin' somewhat. Metzker said, "Stand aside, hayseeds, let a gentleman through," and he musta bumped Armstrong who fell down onto the ground. Quick as a flash, both fellers was up and at him.

MR. FULLERTON: What do you mean "both fellers"?

ALLEN: Armstrong and Norris. Armstrong hit him in the eye with a slingshot, and Norris whacked him in the back of the head with a wagon yoke. Metzker, he went down, and the fight was over just like that.

(FULLERTON picks up a large slingshot from a table and shows it to ALLEN.)

MR. FULLERTON: Is this the slingshot you saw the defendant use to strike Mr. Metzker?

ALLEN: *(studies it for several seconds)* Yessir, it surely is. That is the very one. I reckon.

MR. FULLERTON: Your honor, I mark this weapon, found less than a mile from the scene of the crime just twenty-four hours after Mr. Metzker's death, as Exhibit A, and place it in evidence. Your witness, Mr. Lincoln.

(FULLERTON sits and LINCOLN rises, pacing for several seconds in front of ALLEN, who shifts uneasily.)

MR. LINCOLN: Mr. Allen, was Mr. Metzker still lying on the ground when you left the scene of the fight?

ALLEN: Nosir. Few minutes later, he come to and got up. A couple fellers helped him on his horse, and he rode off toward his home. He was cussin' up a blue streak, too, he was.

MR. LINCOLN: Thank you. That is all.

(LINCOLN turns away, and ALLEN starts to rise; suddenly LINCOLN whirls around and faces ALLEN.)

MR. LINCOLN: One more question, sir: I believe Mr. Fullerton forgot to ask you what time of night it was when the fight occurred. What time was it?

ALLEN: *(settles in witness chair)* Welllll…. it was after midnight.

MR. LINCOLN: Did you look at your watch during the fight?

ALLEN: Don't have no watch. But the camp meetin' was just lettin' out when the fight was the hottest. I heard folks leavin', and the meetin' always let out every night at midnight sharp.

MR. LINCOLN: How far were you from the men while they were fighting?

ALLEN: Fifteen, maybe twenty yards. Close enough, I reckon.

MR. LINCOLN: But you saw everything that happened?

ALLEN: Sure as I'm seein' you right this very minute. The moon made it near light as day.

MR. LINCOLN: Where was the moon, Mr. Allen?

ALLEN: *(points straight up)* Directly overhead. Why, it was so bright I could count the notches on that there slingshot of Duff Armstrong's.

MR. LINCOLN: That was a very bright moon, indeed. No more questions. Defense calls Nelson Watkins.

(ALLEN leaves the stand and shuffles back into his seat next to FULLERTON; NELSON WATKINS takes the stand and is sworn in by BAILIFF.)

MR. LINCOLN: How old are you, Nelson?

WATKINS: Fi-fi-fifteen, sir. Well…fourteen goin' on fifteen.

MR. LINCOLN: And where do you live?

WATKINS: In Menard County. But last summer I was over in Virgin Grove helping my uncle with his wheat harvest.

(LINCOLN picks up the slingshot and shows it to WATKINS.)

MR. LINCOLN: I want you to take a look at this slingshot, son. Ever see it before?

WATKINS: Yessir. I seen it plenty of times. It's mine.

MR. LINCOLN: Yours?

(SPECTATORS murmur; ALLEN shifts uncomfortably; FULLERTON stiffens.)

WATKINS: Yessir. See, it's got my initials on the back of the handle. "N.W."

MR. LINCOLN: It certainly does. When did you last see this?

WATKINS: It fell out of my pocket last summer when my uncle and me was riding through Virgin Grove on the way to Warsaw.

MR. LINCOLN: Do you recall what day you lost your slingshot?

WATKINS: The thirtieth of August. In the morning about noon.

MR. LINCOLN: August thirtieth? That was the day *after* the crime occurred. Less than twenty-four hours, in fact. Why are you so certain of that date, Master Watkins?

WATKINS: Well sir, that's my birthday. And we was on the way to town to get the fixings for a big birthday supper my Aunt Nelda was cooking!

(LINCOLN places slingshot on table and addresses JUDGE HARPER.)

MR. LINCOLN: Thank you, son. You may step down. Judge Harper, I would like to resubmit this piece of "evidence" with the testimony provided by Mr. Watkins as to its ownership—along with the elaborated circumstances of its discovery. And place it as Exhibit A *Minus.*

(SPECTATORS, JURY LAUGH; JUDGE HARPER raps gavel.)

JUDGE HARPER: Have you any more witnesses, Mr. Lincoln?

MR. LINCOLN: Just one, your honor. One more witness, and the defense will rest. And this witness happens to be here in my hat.

(LINCOLN pulls out a small book from the inside of his stovepipe hat and shows it to the JURY, walking around the courtroom and eventually ending up in front of CHARLES ALLEN.)

MR. LINCOLN: It is an almanac. The *Ayres American Almanac* for the year 1857. A very useful little book, containing a great deal of information about our natural world. And it is here in court to prove the state's star witness—is a vile perjurer!

(CROWD gasps, shouts; ALLEN half-rises and is restrained by FULLERTON; JUDGE HARPER smacks gavel several times for order as LINCOLN crosses to JURY.)

MR. LINCOLN: We will call it Exhibit B, and I shall read what it has to say regarding the moon on the night of August twenty-ninth, 1857. "In the middle-western states the moon will set at exactly ten fifty-seven." Gentlemen of the jury: Charles Allen could not have seen by moonlight what he claims he witnessed at the time he claims he witnessed it—at midnight or shortly after.

ALLEN: *(rises)* You're a dang liar!

MR. LINCOLN: *(whirls to face ALLEN)* You, sir, are the liar! *(turns to JURY)* Gentlemen, you have heard the scene of the fight described as occurring in a deep ravine, and that on the west bank of the ravine was a heavy stand of tall oak trees. On the night of August twenty-ninth, the moon had sunk *behind* the trees nearly an hour *before* midnight. It could not possibly have afforded sufficient light to see *anything* ten or even five yards away—much less fifteen or twenty! Not a drunken free-for-all witnessed by a man who admits to an advanced state of inebriation; certainly not the notches on a slingshot Mr. Allen claims to have seen that was, in fact, not even there!

(LINCOLN hands the almanac to the JUDGE and sits down.)

JUDGE HARPER: Court will recess until one o'clock. *(strikes gavel and exits left)*

(JURY follows JUDGE; SPECTATORS stretch and walk around.)

REPORTER: This is incredible! That Lincoln fellow is some razzle-dazzle lawyer. I'm surprised he's not working for some big wealthy law firm in New York.

OLD SOLDIER: I ain't surprised. Why, I knew that man when he was little broth of a boy back in old Kentucky. It was a few years after I fought the British at New Orleans with Andy Jackson, and I was out of work and mighty hungry.

(SPOTLIGHT ON OLD SOLDIER with a knapsack limping forward to center stage; YOUNG ABE LINCOLN enters from right with a fishing pole and a string of fish and doesn't notice OLD SOLDIER.)

OLD SOLDIER: Say there, young feller! You sure got a fine string of fish. Did you catch 'em yourself?

YOUNG ABE LINCOLN: Yessir. Pop didn't think I could catch any fish, but I'll show him. And we'll have a fine big supper!

OLD SOLDIER: Mmmm, supper…why, I haven't had anything to eat for nigh three days.

YOUNG ABE LINCOLN: Gee, in our cabin, we eat twice, sometimes three times every day. Don't you have a home, mister?

OLD SOLDIER: I used to. But I went off to war, and now my family's moved off. Oh, while the war is goin' on, everybody loves the soldier boy, especially the rich fellers that stay home to make all they can out of it. But when the war's over, people treat the soldier done their dirty work like an old worn-out dishrag.

YOUNG ABE LINCOLN: Well, my family isn't that way. Here. You can have my fish. They'll make you a nice supper.

OLD SOLDIER: God bless you, boy. You're a fine little feller. I won't never forget you!

(OLD SOLDIER puts fish in his knapsack and limps back to courtroom seat while YOUNG ABE LINCOLN runs to stage right with his fishing pole where his mother, NANCY LINCOLN, sits sewing. SPOTLIGHT ON NANCY LINCOLN and YOUNG ABE LINCOLN.)

YOUNG ABE LINCOLN: Ma? I caught a mess of catfish in Knob Creek today. And I was bringin' 'em home for supper. But I met an old soldier who hadn't eaten in nigh three days, and I gave the fish to him. All of 'em. I bet everyone will think me a proper fool!

NANCY LINCOLN: *(hugs him)* You done right, Abe, and I'm proud of you. It was right cause it were all you had, and the pride of your soul were in it. And don't worry about what anyone else thinks of a good deed you done. Always remember, it's not what you seem to others, but what you are that counts in this world.

(YOUNG ABE LINCOLN exits right.)

NANCY LINCOLN: My young Abe was always looking out for others. One time at school, some other students were putting fire coals on the backs of turtles. Abe told them to stop, and he fought one boy to make him do so. Now they call him "Honest Abe," and that started when he was a boy, too, when he paid back a man for a book he borrowed but lost—working three weeks clearing stumps at five cents a day to get the money.

(JOSIAH CRAWFORD steps to center stage and addresses REPORTER, who has been taking notes; NANCY LINCOLN exits left.)

JOSIAH CRAWFORD: My name's Josiah Crawford, and I knew Abraham Lincoln when he was a neighbor in Pigeon Creek, Indiana. Oh, he's done some handy lawyering! There was that case back in '41 where the Trailor Brothers were accused of killing an old miser man for his money. The sheriff had their confession and a stick of Bill Trailor's the prosecutor said had the old man's whiskers on it! Well, Abe Lincoln discovered the old man wasn't dead at all; he'd just wandered off for a few days! And the whiskers on Bill Trailor's stick come from an old cow tail! *(laughs)*

(NATHAN CHANDLER walks up and addresses CRAWFORD and the REPORTER, shaking their hands.):

NATHAN CHANDLER: How do, gentlemen—Nathan Chandler of Springfield. When Abe Lincoln was a surveyor round these parts, he saved my land from a swindler. Yessir, when folks were in need, Abe Lincoln was there in deed! Mr. Crawford, do you remember that case involving Matson's slave girl?

JOSIAH CRAWFORD: Back in 1847, wasn't it? A Kentucky slaveowner named Matson had brought a crew of slaves up to Illinois to do some temporary fieldwork. But when it came time to go back South, a slave named Jane Bryant and her children refused. Abe Lincoln proved that, according to the law, all of Matson's slaves had been kept in Illinois illegally and had to be fully emancipated.

(JUDGE HARPER enters courtroom from stage left, sits and strikes gavel.)

BAILIFF: Hear ye, hear ye! Court is now in session!

(SPECTATORS take seats as JURY enters and sits; FULLERTON rises and addresses JURY.)

MR. FULLERTON: Gentlemen of the jury, the state maintains its contention that the overwhelming burden of proof points to the guilt of the accused—in spite of the defense attorney's theatrics. I ask you to render a verdict of guilty as charged.

(FULLERTON bows to JURY and sits. LINCOLN rises slowly and slowly walks to center of courtroom.)

MR. LINCOLN: Gentlemen of the jury, some of you honored me the other day at Springfield by nominating me as your candidate for United States Senator. And some of you, no doubt, can remember twenty-five years back when—as a long lanky youth, penniless and ill-clad—I drifted into Illinois from the Hoosier state…The better part of a man's life consists of his friendships, and there are mighty good friends to be found in these parts. One late fall afternoon, the young man who was me some quarter century ago, had trudged for miles and miles through the wilderness seeking gainful employment, the cold wind beating bitterly through his thin, ill-fitting garments. Suddenly, he heard the cheerful ring of an ax, just as a small cabin loomed into view. The ax belonged to a jolly, stout-handed homesteader, who offered the discouraged boy food and shelter for the evening…Gentlemen of the jury, no king ever met a fellow monarch with a finer welcome. Everything he had, the homesteader told the shivering Abraham, was his. It was only a one-room cabin. Two small children, five and six years of age, played on the dirt floor. A young woman was singing a baby to sleep before the open fire…For many weeks young Abraham Lincoln lived in that cabin, performing a multitude of chores for his room and board. He came to know that family, came to know and cherish them as his own. Came to know the goodness in their hearts, the gentleness in their souls, the rightness of their ways…Gentlemen of the jury, the son of that good man and this poor woman—the baby I often rocked to sleep in its cradle, the young man the State's Attorney has asked you to hang—is no murderer. Part of the testimony against him I have demonstrated to be perjury—the wickedest, most contemptible form of lying. The prosecution has failed utterly to prove that Duff Armstrong was the cause of this unfortunate man Metzker's death. The law of our state, which is also common the world over, specifically says that where death may have been accidental, such as falling from a horse or as the result of self-induced causes, such as alcoholic intoxication, a conviction of murder cannot be sustained.

(He draws out his watch, studies it, holds it forth.)

MR. LINCOLN: In another hour the shadows of night will begin to fall, I do not wish to delay you further in this somber room. If justice be done in this case—and I believe your verdict will be just—before the sun set, it will shine upon my client, a free man. Thank you.

(LINCOLN bows and sits; JURY talk among selves; SWAP addresses REPORTER.)

SWAP: If that isn't the prettiest speechifyin' I ever heard! Say, did you get all that written down?

REPORTER: The meat of it. What do you think of Duff Armstrong's chances now?

SWAP: Well, I'd say that the rumors of his demise have been greatly exaggerated.

REPORTER: *(chuckles)* Say, that's clever. I believe I'll make a note of that. *(writes)*

(JUDGE pounds gavel.)

JUDGE HARPER: Gentlemen of the jury, have you reached a verdict?

JURY FOREMAN: *(rises)* We have, your honor. We find the defendant—not guilty!

(Courtroom erupts in shouts. MRS. ARMSTRONG rushes up to DUFF and hugs him. OLD SOLDIER, NATHAN CHANDLER, JOSIAH CRAWFORD, NELSON WATKINS, DR. BLAKE, JURY MEMBERS and JUDGE congratulate LINCOLN. BAILIFF takes CHARLES ALLEN by arm and leads him offstage left. HUGH FULLERTON shakes his head and addresses LINCOLN.)

MR. FULLERTON: You're awfully sharp, Lincoln. You might go far someday, except for your unfortunate tendency to fight on the side of the underdog.

MR. LINCOLN: Mr. Fullerton, to my way of thinking, that's the only side worth fighting for.

DUFF ARMSTRONG: Mr. Lincoln, you saved my life. I'm forever in your debt.

MR. LINCOLN: Son, I was only repaying a debt of kindess I owed your family for over twenty years. A man must always repay his debts, as long as in doing so he does not compromise his principles.

MRS. ARMSTRONG: I don't know how to thank you, Abe.

MR. LINCOLN: If you were a man, Mrs. Armstrong, I'd ask you to vote for me this fall. But since the Republic hasn't yet seen fit to grant you ladies suffrage, I'll have to settle for a piece of your fresh-baked apple pie next time I come to Mason County.

REPORTER: Mr. Lincoln, based on your success in winning seemingly lost causes, some folks are saying you ought to run for President. Do you have an opinion on that?

MR. LINCOLN: Well now, mister—what did you say your name was?

REPORTER: Clemens, sir. Samuel Clemens.

MR. LINCOLN: Well, Mr. Clemens, given the state of today's political climate, I don't know why anyone in their right mind would want to do a fool thing like that. Run for President? Why, I'd as soon run for President as...well, grow a beard!

(Everyone laughs; LIGHTS OUT.)

THE END

THE SPLENDID VOYAGE OF KITTY DOYLE

Nearly all the millions of people who came to settle in America before the 1950s journeyed by boat. Until the 1880s, when safe, rapid travel by steamship became common, crossing the Atlantic or Pacific Ocean in a sailing vessel of any kind was fraught with peril. Immigrants, in particular, were typically poor and often at the mercy of unscrupulous crews and charter companies. Many thousands of men, women and children seeking a better life in America died on the voyage over of disease, starvation or shipwreck. Several popular ballads of the day described these catastrophes, such as *The New York Trader*, in which a wicked captain admits starving his passengers and stealing from his crew and *The Ship Eliza*, in which a captain deserts his sinking ship and passengers. *The Splendid Voyage of Kitty Doyle* is based on an incident that occurred in 1873 when the White Star Line ship *The Atlantic*, sailing from Liverpool to Halifax, foundered upon rocks with the loss of over 500 passengers. Treachery was suspected, and the captain was suspended for two years.

TIME: Spring Break, the present; March, 1860

PLACE: a jetliner bound for Disneyworld; a steampacket ship sailing from Cork to Boston

CAST: Jennifer/Kitty Doyle   Captain Hiram Blascock
Pieter Zeeman   Navigator Hernandez
First Mate Kramer   Businessman/LeBlanc
Stewardess   Professor/McCloud
Crewmember   A Singer
A Puppy   Young Mother & 3 Young Children
3 Airplane/Ship Passengers
Jennifer's Grandma/Mrs. Mulcahy

STAGE SET: 11 small stools for Passengers at center stage; a rail down right; a table with drawer up right; a helm wheel down left; deck mounts (cubes or platforms) up right and up left with sail rigging behind them

PROPS: paper cup; magazine; knitting needles and knitting; stuffed dog toy; Walkman with headphones; Young Mother's purse; blankets; water bucket; tin cup; swab brush; speaking trumpet; smoking pipe; morsel of bread; coin; earring with bright feather; biscuit; marlin; ledger book; quill pen; *Das Kapital* book; nautical charts; lantern; insurance papers; scalpel in scalpel box; rigging brace; pistol; iron davit; homework book

SPECIAL EFFECTS: sound—intercom static, thunder, lightning, rain and wind sounds, gunshots, boat hull slamming into reef, eight ship bells, jet takeoff noises fading to whispering ocean breezes; visual—lightning flashes

MUSIC: *The Bold Sailor Boy; The Parting Glass; The Ship in Distress;* suggested accompanying instruments—tinwhistle, violin, accordion

COSTUMES: 20th-century characters on airplane wear typical going-to-Florida-for-Spring-Break clothes as described in script, i.e. Stewardess dresses as standard flight attendant, Businessman in suit, etc.; 19th-century ship passengers wear clothes appropriate to their status (impoverished), with Kitty wearing a dress and shawl, women wearing bonnets, men waistcoats and knee breeches; crew wears nautical garb, the Captain attired somewhat more formally

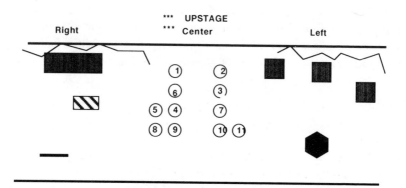

Stage Plan -- *The Splendid Voyage of Kitty Doyle*

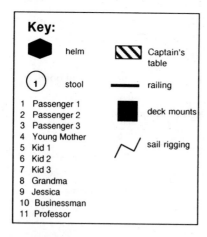

46 The Splendid Voyage of Kitty Doyle

(LIGHTS UP CENTER STAGE, where PASSENGERS sitting in a hot, packed jetliner are becoming increasingly restive as their plane remains motionless on the runway, delayed for over an hour by unexplained computer foulups. BABIES cry, SEATMATES argue, PASSENGERS loosen ties and fidget, waving their emergency cards and barf bags, gulping down water from paper cups and whining to the STEWARDESS as the CAPTAIN'S voice and bad Muzak drone over the speakers. STEWARDESS walking up the aisle from upstage toward downstage stops in front of PASSENGER #1, a kindly-looking old woman.)

CAPTAIN: *(o.s.)* This is your captain welcoming you to Flight 415, non-stop service direct to Orlando, Florida and Disneyworld—

STEWARDESS: And how are we doing here, madam?

PASSENGER #1: *(sweetly)* Honey, we've been doing *here* for over an hour. Do you know what's keeping this plane from making like a bee and buzzing off?

STEWARDESS: Would you care for another cup of water?

PASSENGER #1: *(thrusts her cup at the STEWARDESS)* Gimme a scotch on the rocks and make it a triple!

CAPTAIN: *(o.s.)* —and we're all set for immediate departure sometime in the next—*(static garbles his words)*—and we'll be cruising at an altitude of—*(static)*

PASSENGER #2: *(middle-aged man, fuming, rolling up magazine)* Non-stop? For cryin' out loud, we ain't even started! When we gonna get this hunka junk movin'?

STEWARDESS: *(shuts an overhead latch and looks down at PASSENGER #3, a young man in cowboy hat and mirrored sunglasses)* Sir, would you please secure your seat belt?

PASSENGER #3: *(tips his hat over his eyes and settles back in his seat)* Darlin', I coulda got to Florida faster if I'da rode my mule, Mavis.

CAPTAIN: *(o.s.)* —certainly hope you're enjoying your flight as much as we are—

(A harried YOUNG MOTHER tries frenetically to hush her three sniffling and sneezing YOUNG CHILDREN. In the row in front of them, are JENNIFER and her GRANDMA. The old woman sits calmly and knits, a pleasant smile on her face. JENNIFER is pretty but pouty, fashionably dressed and coiffed in a trendy teen style; she sits on the aisle, frowning and plainly disturbed by the children's ruckus.)

YOUNG MOTHER: (*adjusting her children in their seats and on her lap*) Stephen, don't do that—Marie, no, no, do *not* stick gum in your brother's ear—

MARIE: (*bursts into tears*) Mommy, I got a tummy ache!

YOUNG MOTHER: Michael! Michael! Do not eat your bunny! Ohmygod, you're getting chocolate all over the seats!

STEPHEN: (*wails*) Mommmmmmm! My earrrrrrrr!

YOUNG MOTHER: (*searches in her purse*) Here, honey, I've got some cold medicine in here somewhere, just a minute—Michael! Michael! Marie, stop that! Stephen!

JENNIFER: (*sighs*) Grandma, are we *ever* going to get to Disneyworld? We'll be sitting here my entire spring break!

GRANDMA: Now, Jennifer, just be patient. You're only fourteen years old and you've got a long life ahead of you. Didn't you hear the captain say we'll be taking off in a minute or two?

(*MARIE yowls.*)

JENNIFER: (*to GRANDMA*) I can't hear anything except these little brats! They're driving me nuts!

(*The BUSINESSMAN and PROFESSOR across the aisle erupt into loud argument.*)

BUSINESSMAN: You know, that's what drives me nuts about you namby-pamby do-gooder liberals! Now, take these freeloading welfare cheaters—

PROFESSOR: Welfare, schmelfare! It's the corporate elite and their conniving political lackeys that have bankrupted this country. Have you checked the national debt in the past hour? Four trillion dollars and climbing like a rocket!

BUSINESSMAN: (*loosens his tie and gestures*) If that money hadn't been thrown out the window on all your leftwing so-called art—giving federal grant money for chimpanzees to finger paint in the nude! Our government is funding obscenity!

PROFESSOR: (*wipes his sweaty forehead*) Obscenity! I'll give you obscenity, you want obscenity. It's junk bond hustlers and corrupt savings and loan officers exploiting the middle class! *That's* obscenity, Mr. Wall Street Inside Trader!

BUSINESSMAN: Radical!

PROFESSOR: Warmonger!

BUSINESSMAN: Deviate!

PROFESSOR: Leech!

BUSINESSMAN: Nice meeting you. (*turns away and picks up a finance magazine, looks straight ahead*)

PROFESSOR: Have a nice day. (*turns away and puts on Walkman headphones, stares straight ahead*)

(*JENNIFER shakes her head in amazement, reaches under her seat and pulls out a stuffed dog she picks at idly as the CAPTAIN speaks over the intercom.*)

CAPTAIN: (*o.s. static*) Ladies and gentlemen, we'll be getting underway shortly…possibly…oh, if all goes according to schedule, within the next five minutes to three-quarters of an hour…plenty of time for passengers making connecting flights…

(*PASSENGERS groan, BABIES scream*)

PASSENGER #1: Stewardess! There's no more toilet paper! Hellllllllp!

GRANDMA: (*looks down at JENNIFER'S stuffed dog*) Oh, that's a lovely puppy. Where did you get it?

JENNIFER: (*grimaces*) Kevin Kuppelham. He's in my homeroom. He thinks it means he's going to be my boyfriend or something. As if! (*she pops a stick of neon-green licorice in her mouth*)

GRANDMA: Well, he's very thoughtful.

JENNIFER: (*makes throat-gagging motion*) Grandma, he's a dweeb! His parents work in some kind of factory somewhere on the Southside. I think they even *live* near there, too.

GRANDMA: They used to have some lovely little bungalows on the Southside. That's where I first met your grandfather, at a USO social. He was too nervous to dance, so he kept buying me orange juice all night just to keep us talking. We had to walk home because neither of us had fifteen cents for the trolley.

JENNIFER: (*smiles dreamily*) I want Brandon Webster for my boyfriend. His parents have a humongous house in Fox Grove with an indoor *and* outdoor pool, and his older brother has a cool yellow Jaguar and got accepted to the most expensive private boarding school in the state. They're really neat people; they have real big parties, and they even have maids and butlers and gardeners—you know, menial servant drudge types.

GRANDMA: I worked for a family in Fox Grove once. They were far from neat. In fact, I spent most of my time picking up after the grownups as well as the children.

JENNIFER: (*twists her dog's ears and sighs loudly*) I wish mom could be going with us. Or even dad. Why do *they* always have to be on a business trip when *I* want to go somewhere fun? It's like being an orphan. Ooohhh! Grandma, I'm bored!

GRANDMA: You know, this would be a good time to get some of your homework for school finished.

JENNIFER: No! I'm on spring break! I'm not going to do *any* homework!

GRANDMA: Would you like to try a crossword puzzle?

JENNIFER: (*groans*) Ooh, yuck, Grandma! All those words! Why aren't we moving?

(The CHILDREN behind them start crying loudly.)

JENNIFER: (*to GRANDMA through gritted teeth*) If those little brats don't shut up, I am going to totally lose it!

GRANDMA: Ah, child, what would Grandma Kitty think about all your bussfudgeting? I daresay she'd have something to say about it and it would be something you'd be sure to remember!

JENNIFER: Who's Grandma Kitty? I don't have any grandma named Kitty.

GRANDMA: Grandma Kitty was *my* grandmother. Kathleen Bridget Theresa Doyle was her full name, though everyone just called her Kitty. She'd be great-great-grandmother to you.

JENNIFER: Was she from Ireland?

GRANDMA: Indeed, she was. Did you never hear the story of when she first came to America?

(JENNIFER shakes her head "no"; GRANDMA continues to talk as LIGHTS FADE OUT)

GRANDMA: Well, then…it was in 1860, toward the end of March in a very fine spring, when young Kitty Doyle began her splendid voyage across the wide Atlantic…She was fourteen years old, same as you, and she was having the biggest adventure of her life. She was sailing on her very first ship, The Star of Copenhagen, an old-time steam-packet bound for Boston. Her parents had both died of a sickness two months before, and all Kitty Doyle had in the whole wide world were the clothes on her back, some bits of food she'd saved up before leaving Cork Harbor, and a wee stray puppy she'd found running loose on the docks.

(During blackout, CAST MEMBERS shed modern clothing, don 19th-century garb; sounds of PASSENGERS wailing, CHILDREN crying)

CHILDREN: Food! Food! Mommy, I want food!

PASSENGERS: It's the fever! Give us water! Please, water!

GRANDMA: Oh, and she had Mrs. Mulcahy, a widow lady and a neighbor of the Doyle family back home in Connemara who was making the trip to America with her.

(LIGHTS UP ON FULL STAGE; the airplane interior is now the interior of a ship's hold filled with ragged, malnourished, consumptive emigrants huddled on the floor. Stools are gone, replaced by blankets which PASSENGERS sit on and huddle in. JENNIFER (now KITTY) sits on the floor at front, cradling a small skinny puppy that squirms in her arms, and looking at MRS. MULCAHY, seated next to her sewing some pieces of cloth and humming lightly. A burly CREWMEMBER enters and doles out brackish water to begging PASSENGERS.)

CREWMEMBER: So you want a bleedin' bit of water, do you?

PASSENGER #1: *(the OLD WOMAN, holding out a tin cup in one hand and a coin in her other)* Please, sir, please. I haven't got any left; it's all gone bad.

CREWMEMBER: Aye, granny, you'll get plenty of fresh water if you hop overboard! *(laughs cruelly)* That'll be five pence, thank you. *(grabs coin and sloughs a few gulps of water into the cup)*

PASSENGER #2: *(MIDDLE-AGED MAN, on his knees, tugs at CREW-MEMBER'S sleeve)* Sir, how long have we been becalmed? How many days has it been since the wind died? It's been more than a week, hasn't it? Maybe two? Three, god help us all?

CREWMEMBER: *(roughly shakes him away, and the man falls back)* Blast you, you landgrubbing swab-mite! We're 45 degrees north and 35 west—smack in the deep, black, briny heart of the Devil's Own Latitudes, where the sun don't shine, and the doldrums last for weeks and weeks on end, and there's nobody but the sharks to hear your last miserable wailing cries of mercy to the god what's forsook your cringing yellow-bellied soul the day you were bleedin' born! (*doffs his cap and leers*) And may I offer you some refreshment, sir?

(*CAPTAIN HIRAM BLASCOCK enters from left with a speaking trumpet in his hand; NAVIGATOR HERNANDEZ and FIRST MATE KRAMER enter behind him.*)

CAPTAIN BLASCOCK: (*shouts through the trumpet*) G'day, all you fine Christian ladies and gentlemen, and may the good lord bless your merry souls for traveling with the Red Boar Line. I am Hiram Blascock, your captain for the voyage to Boston. As some of you sharper sea tacks might have surmised, our cruising speed has gotten a trifle sluggish the last few days.

PASSENGER #3: (*MAN, the cowboy now dressed in Greek shepherd's outfit*) Mega kakon! I could have already been to Boston and back to Thermopoli with my goat, Demetrius, who moves at speed of blind snail! And does not know even how to swim like boat!

CAPTAIN BLASCOCK: (*motions to HERNANDEZ*) Our fine navigator, Señor Hernandez, assures me we are directly on course and schedule. Now, if you'll give me leave, I've got a ship to sail.

PASSENGERS: Food! Give us food! We need bread! Give us more water!

(*CREWMEMBER shoves them back.*)

CAPTAIN BLASCOCK: Calm yourselves, calm yourselves. All the employees of the Red Boar Shipping Line are at your service. If you have need of assistance, or have a concern about the quantity of rations, please consult First Mate Kramer. (*motions to KRAMER and bows to PASSENGERS*) G'day!

(*CAPTAIN BLASCOCK turns and exits left, followed by HERNANDEZ and KRAMER and the CREWMEMBER as PASSENGERS mumble; a YOUNG MOTHER and her three sniffling and sneezing YOUNG CHILDREN sprawl forward on blankets in front of KITTY and MRS. MULCAHY, the children crying and tossing restlessly on the floor while the mother tries without success to soothe them. The BUSINESSMAN (now LEBLANC) and PROFESSOR (now McCLOUD) across the aisle erupt into loud argument.*)

LEBLANC: Mon dieu, monsieur McCloud! You and your democracy of les masses! Your kind have ruined mon belle France with these silly notions of freedoms and rights! And now you want to set the African slaves of America running wild cross the continent? Where will you stop with this madness, monsieur? Where will you stop!

McCLOUD: Aye, mister LeBlanc, it's your kind that have made the machine your new god and the factory your new temple of Mammon. You've sold your soul and the spirit of the working class for a scurvy thirty pieces of silver!

LEBLANC: I protest, monsieur! It is the nature of an aristocracy, and an aristocracy is indeed quite naturelle and necessary in the scheme of the development of the state—

McCLOUD: "The state shall wither away of its own accord." That's from Karl Marx, sir, the greatest philosopher and social prophet of our day.

LEBLANC: Marx? Marx? Is he German? Oui! If he is German, then he is quite mad, I assure you, quite mad—

(MRS. MULCAHY touches KITTY'S shoulder.)

MRS. MULCAHY: Kitty, here's a morsel of bread. Why don't you go take it up to that poor Polish family there. They look awfully hungry, don't you think?

KITTY: Then may I go up on deck?

MRS. MULCAHY: If you bundle your cloak tight so you don't catch your death of pneumonia. And don't stray too close to the railing, love. Here, hand over that wee beast.

(KITTY gives the puppy to MRS. MULCAHY and takes the bread to the THREE CHILDREN and their MOTHER who gesticulates her thanks.)

YOUNG MOTHER: Thank you. Thank much. Very much thank.

(KITTY heads upstage, picking her way slowly through the PASSENGERS and comes downstage left, where she climbs out of the hold and ventures onto the main deck, deserted except for a sleeping CREWMEMBER at left, whom she tiptoes carefully around. LIGHTS OUT CENTER AND LEFT, SPOTLIGHT UP RIGHT as KITTY crosses to the railing at stage right and stares out at the ocean.)

GRANDMA: *(o.s.)* It was the first time Kitty had been up on deck since the boat had left Cork Harbor. The night was dark with a new moon and a scattering of stars above. The air was salty and tickled her nose, and she could hear the waves slap up against the hull. She gazed out at the immense ocean that surrounded her—so much water! Yet it was an ocean that was as calm and as motionless as the tranquil blue waters of Lough Graney, where she had spent many a day with her mother and father watching graceful swans and frisky ducks frolic on the shore. The ocean chill made her shiver, and she looked back—toward the east—back toward the home she would likely never see again...

(PIETER ZEEMAN, the cabin boy, has entered from left and creeps up behind KITTY; he touches her shoulder, and she is startled, letting out a small scream as she whirls around.)

KITTY: Aiiiii!

PIETER: Ha! Ha! Ha! Scared you! Scared you!

KITTY: How dare you! Saints above, who do you think you are!

PIETER: I'm Pieter Zeeman, ship's bosun, and I know who you are.

KITTY: Who am I so?

PIETER: You're Miss Scaredy-Cat!

KITTY: Am not!

PIETER: Are so! You almost jumped over the rail!

KITTY: I never!

PIETER: Did so! And then it would have been my duty to save you!

KITTY: Your duty! What duties have the likes of you? Creeping up to young girls and working peculiar mischief?

PIETER: (*puffs out his chest, adjusts his cap*) Why, I've got all kinds of duties. I heave-to the mizzen mast each daybreak. And I set the helmsman on course at nightfall. And I keep the lads tight on their riggings whenever we meet foul weather.

KITTY: (*walks around him, critically*) Go on, you're joking! You're not ship's bosun at all. I saw you when I came aboard. You're the cabin boy.

PIETER: (*flustered*) I said I was the bosun's *mate!* I'm his mate!

KITTY: You're Captain Blascock's cabin boy!

PIETER: Am not!

KITTY: You're a funny-faced wee cabin monkey!

PIETER: You're Miss Scaredy-Cat!

KITTY: Cabin monkey! Cabin monkey!

PIETER: Scaredy-Cat! Scaredy-Cat! Scaredy-Cat!

KITTY: (*turns and begins to walk away left*) A *real* bosun wouldn't speak to a girl in that tone of voice.

PIETER: (*scrambles up beside her*) I can show you around the ship. I'll wager you've never been on a big merchantman like this before.

KITTY: (*stops and looks at him haughtily*) How would you know where I've been or what I've seen?

PIETER: Follow me! I'll show you the foc'sle first!

(LIGHTS UP FULL as PIETER takes KITTY around the ship, scampering back and forth across the stage to the rigging, the helm, etc. and pointing and miming nautical work motions as the song, "The Bold Sailor Boy" is sung.)

SINGER:

As I roved out one evening fair
It being in the spring to take the night air
I spied a bold sailor and a lady so gay
And I stood near to listen to what they would say

They walked 'long the main deck for an hour or two
When from his tote satchel a bright whistle he drew
He played her a ditty that made the sea ring
"Hark! Hark!" cried the lady, "Hear the nightingales sing!"

Now there's many a young lassie has gone from her home
Her fortune to seek, cross the ocean she'll roam
Hoping for fair skies, long life and true joy
Singing the song of her bold sailor boy

(During the last verse PIETER takes a biscuit from the sleeping CREWMEMBER'S satchel and gives it to KITTY; they cross to the railing, KITTY nibbling a biscuit and PIETER tying knots in a small piece of rope.)

KITTY: That was grand, altogether, Pieter! And the biscuit is delicious, too!

PIETER: I can get you an orange tonight. And maybe a lime. The cook turns in at seven bells, and I know where he hides the fruit and rum.

KITTY: I've never seen such a grand lot of ropes and sails and pulleys and watch-you-may-callems in all my life!

PIETER: And there's plenty more you haven't seen yet. The Star of Copenhagen is the best-rigged packet ship I've sailed in all my six years before the mast.

KITTY: Six years! You've been a wee cabin boy since you were eight years old?

PIETER: (*stops threading the rope, glares at her*) Eight? You must be daft! I'm eight-*teen*. Very nearly twenty!

KITTY: (*giggles and swallows the rest of her biscuit*) Pieter Zeeman, you're not a week older than myself, nor an inch taller, and I just turned fourteen Friday week.

PIETER: I'm eighteen!

KITTY: Fourteen!

PIETER: Eighteen!

KITTY: Fourteen!

PIETER: Well...sixteen...

KITTY: Fifteen and not a day more!

PIETER: All right, then...I'll be fifteen the tenth of next month.

KITTY: (*turns away smugly, with a great flounce of her dress*) And I suppose you want me to believe you've been on the high seas for six long years?

PIETER: Well, it's true! I stove away on a merchantman bound for Malta when I was eight. Four days out of Amsterdam they found me and made me the bosun's 'prentice.

KITTY: (*skeptically*) The bosun's 'prentice?

PIETER: Well...the cook's helper. But I *was* eight!

KITTY: And what did your mother and da do when they caught you? Probably gave you the caning of your life!

PIETER: (*turns away*) My parents are dead. My two brothers and I...we lived in an orphanage in Rotterdam. We ran away one night. They were caught, but I got away. And I haven't been back on land since! What about your parents? Are they already in America?

KITTY: No. I have no family, either. They've...that is, my parents, they...they

PIETER: I'm sorry. Here. (*fishes in his jacket pocket and pulls out a large silver earring with a brightly-colored feather*) Look at this.

KITTY: (*takes it and turns it in her palm*) What is it?

PIETER: It's a good-luck charm. A condor feather, see. From the jungles of Ecuador. It brings fair skies and smooth waters as long as you keep it.

KITTY: And where did you get it?

PIETER: From a coxswain's 'prentice in Lisbon. I traded him a Barbary gambler's charm for it.

KITTY: It's beautiful!

PIETER: You can take it. I've got plenty more curios like that. When I become a captain of my own ship, I'll keep a whole trunk full of them.

KITTY: Captain of your own ship!

PIETER: (*struts*) That's right. When I signed on with Captain Blascock two years ago, he said he'd teach me everything there is to know about being a line captain by the time I was sixteen.

KITTY: And what will you do then?

PIETER: (*snorts*) Then I'll get my own vessel, of course! My own frigate with a top-rank line like the Red Boar or White Cross or Black Diamond.

KITTY: And you'll be spending the rest of your life drifting from wave to wave? Bathing in salt spray and eating hard tack and corn dodger?

PIETER: (*ignores her*) And I'll sail to the Orient and bring back spices and emeralds and silk. And I'll buy a ship of my own, a ship like The City of Baltimore—two thousand tons of beauty and speed, all painted gold and white and silver with the highest top sail in the line!

KITTY: (*giggles*) Then you can buy a whole fleet!

PIETER: Yes! Yes! I'll buy a whole fleet! Freighters! Passenger ships! And merchantmen that can sail round Cape Horn from New Orleans to Buenos Aires in seven weeks!

KITTY: You can't sail round Cape Horn from New Orleans to Buenos Aires in seven weeks!

PIETER: (*turns and faces her, standing on his tiptoes to be taller*) Can so!

KITTY: Can not!

PIETER: Why not!

KITTY: Because New Orleans and Buenos Aires are both on the same side of Cape Horn. They're both on the Atlantic side!

PIETER: Are not!

KITTY: Are so!

PIETER: How would you know? You've never been anywhere away from your old Irish potato farm! *I've* sailed the ocean!

KITTY: And *I've* had lessons in geography! I can read maps!

PIETER: (*points up in sky*) And I can read the stars and know where I am anywhere in the world! Sure, I can read letters right enough. But what good does a bunch of hen scratches and fly specks do a person when he's in the middle of a raging gale on the high sea? Or when he has to tie down a halyard sail in the dark dead of night?

KITTY: It might keep you from getting lost on the way from New Orleans to Buenos Aires.

PIETER: Awwww—I suppose you're going to spend the rest of your life reading books?

KITTY: I will, indeed. I plan to be a teacher. Like Mrs. Mulcahy. And I'll read every book worth reading in the entire world. Which is to say, my little Dutchman, every book there *is*.

PIETER: Well...reading books is all right...for girls and women. But they'd only fill a man's head with foolish notions. A man can't learn anything useful from reading a book.

KITTY: Tisn't so!

PIETER: Tis!

KITTY: Tisn't!

PIETER: Tell me one thing *you've* ever read in a book that *I'd* want to know about!

KITTY: (*twirls the condor feather charm around her finger and looks haughtily away*) Something every sailor lad worth his salt should know! *I* can signal the Morse Code.

PIETER: (*guffaws*) *You* know Morse Code? A *girl!* Sure, and I know the whole Bible in Chinese! Backwards!

KITTY: I do, so!

PIETER: And fishes ride camels in the deserts of Mongolia!

KITTY: I'll show you. (*takes the earring and knocks on the railing*) Dot-dash-dash-dot...dot-dot...dot...dash...dot...dot-dash-dot...what's that spell?

PIETER: (*frowns*) It...um, it...let's see—

KITTY: It's your own name—"Pieter." (*knocks*) Dot-dot...dot-dot-dot...dot-dash—"is a"—dash-dot-dot..."D"...dot-dot-dash..."U"...dash-dot..."N"—

PIETER: (*flustered*) That's enough!

KITTY: I learned *that* from a book.

PIETER: And *I'll* learn it from Captain Blascock!

KITTY: When?

PIETER: When he thinks I'm ready to learn it! He's always teaching me important things. And not from an old bunch of books!

KITTY: Can he teach you to get us out of these windless waters?

PIETER: Captain Blascock is a great ship captain. And he's my best friend! We're in no danger.

KITTY: Pieter, the passengers are starving! And sick! That poor Polish family is weak nearly to death from fever! And where is the ship's doctor?

PIETER: The ship's doctor? That's Major Briggs. You saw him in the crew's mess. He served against the Russians in Crimea!

KITTY: He looks like he served against Napoleon at Waterloo!

PIETER: Captain Blascock says he's a fine doctor!

KITTY: (*puts her hands on her hips and stands directly in front of him*) Then why isn't he below with the passengers instead of lolling about the crew's mess with his nose stuck inside a rum cask? What does your precious Captain Blascock say about that?

PIETER: Whatever Captain Blascock says is true, and I believe him!

(CAPTAIN BLASCOCK enters behind them from right, unobserved, carrying a large, curved pipe in his mouth; NAVIGATOR HERNANDEZ and FIRST MATE KRAMER follow behind him.)

KITTY: And if he said we were going to sail up into the twinkling stars and land on the white silvery moon, you'd believe him?

PIETER: I would! And so should you, Miss Smarty-Bloomers! (*shakes his finger at her*)

KITTY: I'm not inclined to believe a man who stands by while small children and old people suffer without decent food and water!

PIETER: You've got no right! (*clenches his fist*) How dare you say a harsh word about the Captain! How dare you—

CAPTAIN BLASCOCK: Zeeman! What's all the commotion?

(PIETER and KITTY whirl around to face him.)

PIETER: Nothing, sir. I mean, Kitty—I mean, the passenger, Mistress Doyle, she, well, she—

KITTY: (*curtsies awkwardly*) I do beg your pardon, Captain Blascock, sir. I lost my way for a moment and your crewman, Master Zeeman, helped put me aright. (*pauses and curtsies again*)

CAPTAIN BLASCOCK: That's why we don't abide passengers above deck. You'll want to stay below if you wish to keep out of harm's way.

KITTY: Yes, sir. (*curtsies again*) I won't, sir. I mean, I will. That is, I won't be in the way.

CAPTAIN BLASCOCK: First Mate Kramer will escort you back to your berth. And now, Master Zeeman, if you're quite done with your frolics, I'll see you back in my quarters straightaway. *(turns around, as KRAMER motions for KITTY to walk left)*

PIETER: Aye, Captain. *(lowers his head)*

KITTY: *(hurries in front of BLASCOCK, blocking his way)* Don't punish him, sir. It wasn't his fault, not any of it.

CAPTAIN BLASCOCK: *(stands back and regards her quizzically)* It's my duty to see the passengers under my protection remain safe and secure for the duration of this voyage. And that my crew obey orders and perform as befits their rank and station. Do you agree, Master Zeeman?

PIETER: Aye, aye, Captain.

CAPTAIN BLASCOCK: Do you see this pipe, Miss Doyle?

KITTY: I do, sir.

CAPTAIN BLASCOCK: Come closer, child. Look at it up close. *(holds it out)*

KITTY: *(steps closer and peers at pipe)* It *is* a pipe, sir.

CAPTAIN BLASCOCK: *(chuckles)* Of course it is, girl. And to look at it now, you might think it's just an ordinary sort of common smoking pipe, wouldn't you?

KITTY: Well, sir—it's a very beautiful pipe. And it has some peculiar markings round the back of the bowl.

CAPTAIN BLASCOCK: Peculiar markings?

KITTY: Oh, sir, I'm sorry, sir, I didn't mean "peculiar" in any impunative manner. It's just that, that—*(peers closer)* these tiny wee markings, they're some sort of letters in an Arabic alphabet, are they not?

CAPTAIN BLASCOCK: They are, indeed. It was obtained in the market of Marrakesh. And, you are very observant, Miss Doyle. The average European man or woman not only would fail to identify the language of the letters, they wouldn't see them as letters at all. Where did you learn to read Arabic?

KITTY: Oh, I don't read Arabic, sir. I just know what it looks like.

PIETER: *(scornfully)* She probably saw it in some book, Captain!

CAPTAIN BLASCOCK: *(sternly)* Master Zeeman!

KITTY: I did, sir. I saw it in a book.

CAPTAIN BLASCOCK: Would you like to know what it says?

KITTY: Yes, sir, I would, please.

CAPTAIN BLASCOCK: It's a proverb, an old one from ancient Mesopotamia. "A fool is known by his laughing, a wise man by the silence that shadows his heart." This pipe is very dear to me. I count it as one of my most valuable possessions.

KITTY: It's very beautiful, sir.

CAPTAIN BLASCOCK: It's more than merely beautiful, Miss Doyle. I believe it an inspiration.

PIETER: An inspiration?

CAPTAIN BLASCOCK: (*turns to PIETER*) Certainly, Master Zeeman. It's an object of beauty and of mystery. Mystery that inspires contemplation about the conduct of our lives, about the folly and wisdom of our very existence on God's green earth. (*turns to the ocean/ audience*) About the majesty of His power and our own destiny to claim our rightful share of His heaven and our paradise. (*clenches his fist*) Claim it from the darkness that hangs o'er every human heart like a shroud into all eternity!

(There is silence for a few moments.)

PIETER: (*awed*) That is mighty powerful speaking, Captain!

CAPTAIN BLASCOCK: Yes. Yes, indeed, this pipe is very dear to me. G'day, Miss Doyle.

KITTY: (*curtsies*) Sir.

(She exits left with KRAMER following behind her; PIETER exits right followed by HERNANDEZ. CAPTAIN BLASCOCK leans against railing, chewing the pipe; he calmly knocks the ashes out of his pipe, chuckles, then laughs heartily and flings the pipe overboard.)

(LIGHTS OUT BRIEFLY THEN UP FULL as "The Ship in Distress" is sung and played on a tinwhistle or fiddle or accordion.)

SINGER:
Twas two hundred migrant pilgrims crossing the white Atlantic foam
Adrift upon the raging sea so far from hearth and home
The weather proved to them so cruel, their suffering sad to see
With lives in trust to wicked men, they sailed toward misery

(During song, PIETER tightens sail rigging upstage right, waves to KITTY as she watches from up center. PIETER climbs down and exits back right as KITTY'S attention is drawn to down left where FIRST

MATE KRAMER and a CREWMEMBER haul aboard a giant marlin; she creeps closer, hides behind a stool and watches them as they tote it up left and offstage. She then looks across stage and watches PIETER enter from right carrying a swab bucket; he notices NAVIGATOR HERNANDEZ and CAPTAIN BLASCOCK at the CAPTAIN'S table, studying a map and conversing furtively; PIETER listens, then knocks at the door, and BLASCOCK hurriedly shoves the map into his table drawer. Song ends; LIGHTS OUT BRIEFLY, THEN UP AGAIN CENTER ONLY as PASSENGERS lay disconsolately around hold: the Polish MOTHER sits with one CHILD at her feet, one in her lap and another cuddled against her breast, the CHILDREN crying, coughing and sneezing, tears trickle from the mother's eyes; McCLOUD reads from a large dusty tome—"Das Kapital"—while LEBLANC adds sums in a ledger book, entering them with a stylish quill pen. KITTY and MRS. MULCAHY sit, MRS. MULCAHY sewing and lightly humming the tune of "The Bold Sailor Boy," while KITTY stares ahead intently, frowning as she listens to the cries of the FAMILY in front. The puppy lays asleep at her side.)

GRANDMA: *(o.s.)* The storm that blew in that night brought a fine welcome wind that pushed The Star of Copenhagen out of the doldrums and back on her course to Boston. Yet even so, the ship was still at the mercy of fickle winds and frivolous currents. The emigrants in steerage below often wondered if they ever would see the golden shores of America.

McCLOUD: *(points to FAMILY)* Good God, man, take a look over there! The crowning glory of your devil-snatch-the-hindmost free market economic system. These piteous innocents are suffering the torments of Hell on Earth a mere five feet away. Have you no shame? Have you no heart?

LEBLANC: Thirty-three thousand francs; thirty-four thousand francs—quel? Mais non, monsieur, mais non! These good people are not "victims" of an unresponsive society; they are, how do you say, "expendables" of our progressive social system. *(shrugs)* They come, they go. Here today, gone tomorrow. And who shall miss them? Shall you, monsieur?

McCLOUD: They are human beings, sir. But to you, they're nothing more than numbers in a ledger book! And you call that progress?

LEBLANC: But we are not so very different, you and I. (*taps his ledger with his quill*) I devote my life to books filled with tiny numbers, while you…(*points with quill to McCLOUD'S tome*) to books exploding with grand, earth-shaking ideas. So tell me, monsieur: when all *my* numbers are counted and all *your* ideas pronounced, do they ever make the slightest difference in the lives of your darling innocents?

McCLOUD: (*turns away, opens book, mutters*) Blackguard.

LEBLANC: (*picks up quill, sighs*) Reprobate.

McCLOUD: (*reads along with finger*) Unconscionable rapscallion.

LEBLANC: (*writes in ledger*) Communistic wastrel.

McCLOUD: Incorrigible knave.

LEBLANC: Insufferable rogue.

KITTY: (*leans close to MRS. MULCAHY and speaks in a low voice*) Do you think we ever shall reach our destination, Mrs. Mulcahy?

MRS. MULCAHY: (*pauses in her sewing*) That's not for us to know, my dear, is it now? If the rations hold and we get some good fresh wind, I'd say we shall. (*glances at the POLISH FAMILY*) Though I do worry about some of us.

KITTY: The crew has plenty of food! They're cheating the passengers and pretending there's no food, but there is! There is!

MRS. MULCAHY: (*resumes sewing*) Now, now, Kitty—your imagination is getting the better of you, girl. That sounds like some story you read in one of your fairytale books.

KITTY: (*scrambles to her knees*) But it's true! Yesterday they caught a huge big fish! And I saw where the cook keeps extra rations hidden away!

MRS. MULCAHY: Why don't you be a nice helpful lass and let these children have a go with your wee puppy. Go on, be a good lass.

KITTY: Yes, ma'am.

(*She picks up the dog and hands it to the YOUNG MOTHER.*)

YOUNG MOTHER: This, what is? For us this is?

KITTY: Yes, ma'am. For you and your wee ones.

YOUNG MOTHER: (*smiles and wakes her CHILDREN*) Stefan! Miklos! Marica! Thank much! Very for us!

(*The CHILDREN rise and play with the dog, as KITTY waves goodbye to it; she walks slowly through the sleeping passengers to the front of the hold and up onto the main deck down left as "The Parting Glass" is sung.)*

SINGER:
> Oh, all the comrades I ever had
> They're sorry for my going away
> And all the sweethearts I ever knew
> They'd wish me one more day to stay
> But since it falls upon my lot
> That I should rise and you should not
> I gently rise and softly call
> "Good night and joy be with you all"

(KITTY stands on deck, looking out at the ocean; when song ends, she hears a loud thump, cries out and whirls to face it.)

KITTY: Who's there?

PIETER: (*emerging from behind her*) Ah-ha! Miss Scaredy-Cat scared of her own shadow! You know Captain Blascock doesn't allow passengers above deck at night.

KITTY: Yes, and I know Captain Blascock is allowing the passengers to starve to death before we reach Boston!

PIETER: Starve! How can you say that? We're all on short rations, even the crew. I myself have not had more than three biscuits and a bowl of cornmeal a day since Tuesday last.

KITTY: Not *all* the crew, Pieter. I saw the cook hoarding food in a secret closet, and I'm sure he has more hidden away. (*she turns away and walks left*)

PIETER: Say! Where do you think you're going?

KITTY: (*without turning*) I'm going to find the hidden food. The food the passengers should be getting. The food your Captain Blascock is keeping for himself.

PIETER: (*runs up and grabs her wrist*) You can't do that! You'll be caught and severely punished!

KITTY: (*pulls away*) People are starving, Pieter! Starving to death! Someone has to do something!

PIETER: (*laughs nervously*) No. That is not true. Captain Blascock would not let that happen. Why, just two days ago we caught a big marlin, and he ordered First Mate Kramer to dress it and give it to the passengers. I heard him say so with my own ears.

KITTY: And *I* saw Kramer carry it to the galley, and *I* saw the cook hide it. No passengers got any part of that fish, Pieter. Not a one!

PIETER: I don't believe it! And what were you doing up on deck without escort?

KITTY: (*turns her head slightly away and softens her voice*) Perhaps I came to see you, Pieter.

PIETER: Me? You came to see me?

KITTY: Well…perhaps. Perhaps yes and perhaps no.

PIETER: And what did you want to see me about?

KITTY: I didn't say I *wanted* to see you. I said *perhaps* I just wanted to *see* you. There *is* a difference, you know.

PIETER: (*removes his cap and scratches his head*) Just wanted to see me? But you know what I look like. What did you want to see? Did you think I'd sprouted wings and could fly? (*spreads his arms like a chicken and laughs*)

KITTY: Silly! It's not *what* I wanted to see. It's, it's—oh, if you were *really* fifteen years old, you'd understand what a girl wants to see!

PIETER: (*he throws up his arms*) If I live to be a *hundred* and fifteen I'll never *ever* understand women! Or *girls!*

KITTY: (*she comes close beside him*) Sure, what is there to understand? A girl only wants to be happy. Isn't that what everyone wants?

PIETER: (*scratches his head*) I'd say so. But I want to be happy in my own way.

KITTY: Your own way?

PIETER: That's right. I want to spend my life on the open sea. Away from people and their crowded dirty cities and all the things they do to make themselves unhappy.

KITTY: I'd get lonely being on a boat all by myself in the middle of nothing but water.

PIETER: Not I! If I could just be alone on the ocean every day of my life, I'd be the happiest person in the world! Weren't you happy when you lived on your farm in the countryside? Nobody to bother you. Nobody to see for miles and miles. Ah, that's the life for me!

KITTY: (*sighs*) The country was nice enough. But I love to be around people. Lots and lots of people. I love to hear them talk and laugh and shout and cry even—it means they're feeling something deep inside their hearts and souls. (*she reaches out with her hands in the air*) Oh, Pieter! Can't you hear it?

PIETER: (*cups his hand over his ear*) Hear what?

KITTY: Hear the sound of all the hearts all around us! They're everywhere! All over the world! When I get to Boston, Pieter, I'm going to set out and find the biggest city with the most people in all of America—New York, Philadelphia, St. Louis, Charleston. Wherever it is, I'll live there in the very center of it where I can hear thousands of millions of hearts beating every minute of the night and day.

PIETER: (*takes her hand in his*) May I escort you back to your berth, Mistress Kitty?

KITTY: (*jumps away, still holding his hand*) Goodness, no! We've got to get food for the passengers!

PIETER: You can't! Captain Blascock forbids it!

KITTY: I don't care what Captain Blascock forbids! We've got to do something! Come on! (*pulls him along left*)

PIETER: (*pulls back and stops her*) I can't. It's against my orders. (*drops her hand and stands at attention*) My orders are to not allow any passengers above deck.

KITTY: (*squares toward him, hands on her hips*) Is that so, Pieter Zeeman? Your orders are to let innocent people suffer in fever and misery?

PIETER: No! My orders are to—

KITTY: If you carry out your orders, people will starve to death! Your orders are wrong!

PIETER: (*shakes his head, raises his finger*) No, these are Captain Blascock's orders!

KITTY: Then Captain Blascock's orders are wrong!

PIETER: I have served the Captain for two years. He has been like a father to me. And my teacher and my best friend. If he gives an order, it is a good order, and it is my duty to carry it out!

KITTY: Was that what you were thinking yesterday in the cockpit?

PIETER: What?

KITTY: I saw you hiding and watching the Captain. What was he saying that turned you so pale, my little Dutchman?

PIETER: I…I…I don't know…I mean, I didn't understand…he was saying something to the Navigator about changing course…

KITTY: Changing course? To where?

PIETER: I don't know! I couldn't hear everything they said, but they were looking at charts...something about Cape Canso and Chedabucto Bay...places I'd never heard of, but—

KITTY: Oh, fiddlesticks! We're wasting time! Are you coming to help me or not?

PIETER: My orders...Captain Blascock's orders—

KITTY: Listen to *my* orders, Master Zeeman! People are suffering, and we've got to stop it. You can do what your Captain tells you—or what your conscience tells you.

PIETER: No! I...I...I don't know...I—

KITTY: (*steps toward him*) Pieter...I need your help. Please.

(*Noise from the other side of the stage bursts out—a blast of raucous music and laughter from some drunken crewmen. KITTY and PIETER crouch low and watch until the door closes. They look at each other, then PIETER pulls her up and starts toward the galley.*)

PIETER: Come on. The deck watchman is up at six bells. And be quiet. If you drop so much as a biscuit we'll be keelhauled.

KITTY: (*squeezes his arm*) You're a good lad, Pieter Zeeman. May you be safe already in heaven before the Devil knows you're dead.

PIETER: Aach! I will never understand girls or women if I live to be a *thousand* and fifteen!

(*They tiptoe left across stage and exit left. SOUND CUE: eight bells toll the hour of midnight; LIGHTS OUT BRIEFLY, THEN UP AGAIN RIGHT as CAPTAIN BLASCOCK stands at his table, poring over shipping charts and legal documents. There is a knock at the door, and he rolls up the charts and places them over the papers. PIETER enters from right, his cap missing and his clothes bedraggled.*)

CAPTAIN BLASCOCK: Enter.

PIETER: (*steps up to table*) You wanted to see me, Captain?

CAPTAIN BLASCOCK: Aye, lad, come in. By the deuce, you look like you've just swum the Straits of Malabar and back!

PIETER: Begging your pardon, Captain, sir. One of the flybridge riggings tore loose, and I only now finished putting her right.

CAPTAIN BLASCOCK: Good lad! You'll make a line captain sooner than you think. Master Zeeman. Pieter. You've served with me nearly two years now, is it?

PIETER: Aye, sir. Two years, two months, twelve days and four hours.

CAPTAIN BLASCOCK: (*chuckles*) Accurate to the T. That's a fine quality for a sea captain to have. (*opens the table drawer and pulls out a narrow black box*) It's also an enviable quality in a surgeon.

PIETER: A surgeon, Captain?

CAPTAIN BLASCOCK: Aye, lad. A surgeon. (*pushes box across the table*) Open it.

(*PIETER opens the box; he takes out an ornately engraved, silver-handled scalpel and holds it aloft.*)

CAPTAIN BLASCOCK: That's a surgeon's scalpel, a tool that comes in very handy on the operating table.

PIETER: It's…it's magnificent!

CAPTAIN BLASCOCK: It belonged to my son, Jonathan.

PIETER: Your son?

CAPTAIN BLASCOCK: He was enrolled in the Glasgow School of Medicine when a fever took him. His mother, too, my wife. It's the only item of his I've kept all these years. I want you to have it. It will stand you in good stead during your own studies.

PIETER: My own studies? Sir?

CAPTAIN BLASCOCK: When we arrive in Boston, we'll find a proper ship's doctor and apprentice you to him straight away. You're far too clever a lad to be a mere ragamuffin rig-jammer all your life. You need a stable trade, boy—a trade that applies your innate curiosity and knowledge to the limit.

(*PIETER is stunned and silent; his face betrays a flurry of intense emotion.*)

CAPTAIN BLASCOCK: Go on, lad. Take it. It'll prove an inspiration in the coming years.

(*PIETER turns the scalpel over and runs his fingers along the engraving.*)

PIETER: It's a wonder, sir. It truly is. How shall I ever repay you?

CAPTAIN BLASCOCK: Keep it as a reminder of our time together before the mast. I can only hope—

(*FIRST MATE KRAMER and NAVIGATOR HERNANDEZ enter from right and enter CAPTAIN'S cabin.*)

FIRST MATE KRAMER: Herr Captain! Herr Captain! Come quick! We've passed Breton Point!

NAVIGATOR HERNANDEZ: (*restrains him*) Hold on, mate. The Captain's busy.

CAPTAIN BLASCOCK: As you were, gentlemen. Master Zeeman, if you'll tidy up in the corner there and see to my day uniform for tomorrow, I'll attend to this matter and return shortly.

PIETER: Very good sir.

(*BLASCOCK, KRAMER and HERNANDEZ cross stage and exit left. PIETER stares at the scalpel, shakes his head in wonder and puts it back in its box on the table. He straightens papers on the desk and whistles "The Parting Glass"; he accidentally knocks over some papers and picks them up, placing them on the table; he turns away, then turns back and picks up one of the papers.*)

PIETER: (*reading*) "Conditions of Resti...tution, Tarbert & Sons, Limited, London, Maritime Underwriters...the party of the second part...in the happenstance of sinkage...loss of vessel...other natural disaster...agrees to...will be com...com...com-pen-sa-ted...two hundred fifty thousand pounds! Two hundred fifty thousand—"

(*PIETER replaces paper on desk and grabs rolled-up charts. He spreads them out on desk and studies them.*)

PIETER: No! I don't believe it! I must speak to the Captain!

(*BLASCOCK, KRAMER and HERNANDEZ re-enter from left and begin to cross to right, mumbling. PIETER puts the paper he was reading in his jacket backs away from the table and starts for the door. He stops, turns and sees the scalpel still on the table; he goes over, closes the box lid, puts it under his arm and exits right as LIGHTS GO OUT BRIEFLY, THEN UP CENTER as the PASSENGERS sleep.*)

KITTY: (*sits up and shakes herself awake*) No! No! No! (*opens her eyes*) Oh, Mrs. Mulcahy, what a dreadful dream I just had! Mrs.—

(*She starts to cry out and PIETER'S hand closes over her mouth, his index finger over his lips to indicate quiet.*)

PIETER: Hush, now. Hush and come with me. Quickly. There's no time to lose.

KITTY: Come where? What are you doing here? Where are your manners, Pieter Zeeman?

PIETER: (*grabs her shoulders*) We changed course yesterday and passed through Cabot Strait off Cape Breton. We're nearly forty leagues northwest of course!

KITTY: Forty leagues? But why? Isn't Boston due south?

PIETER: Don't you see? We're not going to Boston! The ship is going to run aground in the reef banks off Aspy Bay.

KITTY: Run aground? (*she pulls away from his grip*) Saints preserve us!

PIETER: And then scuttled. I saw them loading provisions into the yawl.

KITTY: The yawl? That wee boat? Oh, Pieter! No! That's mutiny! We must warn the Captain!

PIETER: (*takes paper from inside his jacket and shows them to her*) Look at this, Kitty. It's an insurance contract from the ship's agent. If The Star of Copenhagen goes down, she's worth two hundred fifty thousand in gold.

KITTY: (*studies paper*) Where did you get this?

PIETER: (*hesitates*) In Captain Blascock's cabin.

KITTY: Captain Blascock! Pieter, you don't think—

PIETER: I don't know what I think. I mean, I think—oh, blast! There's no time to think! The ship is going to run aground any minute. (*pulls her up*) Come on!

KITTY: Pieter, wait! We must warn the passengers!

PIETER: We can't save them all! There's no time!

KITTY: Mrs. Mulcahy! (*she rouses MRS. MULCAHY*) Mrs. Mulcahy, rise up! Rise up and get everyone on deck! Right away!

MRS. MULCAHY: *(sleepily)* Kitty, darling, what's the matter?

KITTY: The ship's foundering! Mr. McCloud! Monsieur LeBlanc! Help get the passengers out of the hold and above deck!

(*MRS. MULCAHY struggles to her feet, McCLOUD and LEBLANC awake, and murmuring begins among the PASSENGERS. LIGHTS FLASH and PASSENGERS shout with panic, move to up left and crouch near rigging. PIETER grabs KITTY'S hand and pulls her forward.*)

PIETER: Come on!

(PIETER and KITTY run down right to railing. SOUND CUE: wind, rain, thunder, lightning.)

KITTY: *(points out to audience)* Look! The banks! We're headed straight for them!

PIETER: We've got to get to the helm and set her away from the shore!

(They turn left and start running down left, but a CREWMEMBER has entered from left and blocks their path.)

CREWMEMBER: I say, younglings—aren't we up past our beddy-bye time?

(He tries to grab PIETER, who avoids his grasp and kicks him in the shin. He howls, and KITTY kicks him in the other shin. He falls onto the deck and rolls upstage.)

PIETER: He's rolling to the hold!

KITTY: Someone, help us!

(McCLOUD and LEBLANC come up from back, grab and restrain him.)

McCLOUD: We've got him! You get to the helm!

LEBLANC: Mon Dieu! The crew is making for the small boat! Stop them!

(PASSENGERS shout and run to up right, as CREWMEMBER rolls offstage; SOUND CUE: three gunshots. PIETER and KITTY run to the helm; PIETER grabs it, struggling to maneuver a course through the craggy rocks.)

KITTY: We're going to hit the reef!

(SOUND CUE: hull scraping reef; PASSENGERS shout in alarm; PIETER and KITTY nearly fall down.)

PIETER: We're in too close! This storm is driving us on the rocks!

(KITTY sees a lantern behind her and seizes it.)

PIETER: What are you doing with that lantern? It'll go out as soon as it hits the water!

KITTY: I can signal for help! (*she unwraps the shawl from around her waist*)

PIETER: Signal for help? How?

KITTY: Morse Code! (*demonstrates using her shawl to cover and uncover the lantern*) There's a chance someone on shore or another ship might see it and help us!

(*SOUND CUE: hull scraping reef; PASSENGERS shout in alarm; KITTY steadies herself and begins signaling as PIETER struggles with the wheel. CAPTAIN BLASCOCK enters from right and marches toward them.*)

CAPTAIN BLASCOCK: Pieter! Stop! You don't know what you're doing!

PIETER: Stay away! You're mad!

CAPTAIN BLASCOCK: Get away from there! Come with me onto shore!

PIETER: Captain, how could you do this?

CAPTAIN BLASCOCK: I order you to leave the helm at once! Now, lad! Come with me! Come with me! (*reaches out his hand to PIETER*) Come on, son! Come to me! Please! Hurry!

(*SOUND CUE: hull scraping reef; KITTY cries out and falls to her knees.*)

CAPTAIN BLASCOCK: (*points to KITTY*) You! Girl! Put down that lantern! (*advances toward her*)

PIETER: No!

(*PIETER runs at the CAPTAIN, and they struggle, PIETER trying to knock the CAPTAIN off his feet.*)

PIETER: Run, Kitty! Run!

(*KITTY gathers up the lantern and shawl and slips away, exiting left. Another flurry of punches, and the CAPTAIN lands a blow against PIETER'S temple that sends him sprawling and knocks him unconscious. He stares at the boy's limp body for a moment, then draws a pistol from inside his jacket and exits left after KITTY. LIGHTNING FLASH; KITTY re-enters from left, crosses up right, then turns around and moves up left, as shouts of PASSENGERS and CREW are heard. A brace from the rigging up left breaks loose and falls, startling her and causing her to drop the lantern. She stoops to pick it up as CAPTAIN BLASCOCK enters from left; she leaves the lantern and runs up right with BLAS-COCK in pursuit; she hides behind his table.)*

CAPTAIN BLASCOCK: Miss Doyle! I have something to show you. (*brandishes pistol as he paces*) It's an object of beauty. And of mystery. Mystery that inspires contemplation about the conduct of our lives. The folly and wisdom of our very existence on God's green earth. Come, Miss Doyle, let us talk of mystery and beauty. Let us talk of wisdom and folly. And the darkness that hangs over every human heart like a shroud into all eternity! Eternity, Miss Doyle! Eternity! Are you ready for eternity?

(SOUND CUE: hull scraping reef; KITTY cries out and falls to her knees; LIGHTNING FLASH; she rises and CAPTAIN BLASCOCK stands before her, five feet away, his pistol pointed at her.)

CAPTAIN BLASCOCK: A fool is known by her laughing…a wise woman by the silence that shadows her heart. (*laughs*) I proclaim that you are a very wise woman, Miss Doyle. Can you feel the shadows silencing your heart? Silencing it unto all eternity!

(He cocks the hammer, lowers the pistol to laugh at the cowering KITTY, then raises it again. Suddenly, a large iron davit swings through the air and strikes him a glancing blow on the side of the head causing him to drop the pistol and fall to his knees. PIETER, his head bloodied, enters from up right; armed with a scalpel, he jumps between the CAPTAIN and KITTY.)

CAPTAIN BLASCOCK: Ohhhhh, laddie…that was a right smart tap on the noggin…(*he advances on PIETER, who backs up into KITTY*) I'm proud of you…aye, proud I am…proud…

PIETER: Captain, please! Please, don't come any nearer! Captain, please!

(KITTY stands by his side)

CAPTAIN BLASCOCK: Come to me, lad. Don't be afraid. Come to me now.

(He rushes PIETER but slips on the wet deck and loses his balance. He rolls and grabs at PIETER'S feet, missing as the ship lurches and sends

him tumbling backwards toward the edge of stage mid right. He struggles to his knees.)

CAPTAIN BLASCOCK: (*bellowing*) The majesty of His power, lad! Claim your rightful share of paradise!

(SOUND CUE: hull scraping reef; the CAPTAIN falls on his side, and KITTY shoves him in the shoulder with her foot. He loses his grip on the deck, slides, tumbles and with a roar hurtles over the edge into the darkness.)

CAPTAIN BLASCOCK: To paradise!

(PIETER drops scalpel; KITTY and PIETER embrace each other briefly; the PASSENGERS rush up to them, cheering.)

McCLOUD: We've rounded up the whole verminous crew! What about the Captain?

PIETER: (*motioning to the edge of the stage*) He...he sailed away.

LEBLANC: And good riddance to his kind also, yet again, too! Regardez! On the horizon! Lights!

McCLOUD: It's a rescue ship! By thunder, we're saved!

(SOUND CUE: hull scraping reef.)

PIETER: Not yet we're not! Haul down that topgallant! You men there! Clew in the foremast! Hallo, Scotsman—find another lantern and guide that sloop in to us. I need someone to spell me at the helm.

KITTY: (*steps forward*) I can spell you. In Morse Code, at the very least.

(PIETER smiles and takes her hand. She dabs at his bruised temple with the corner of her shawl. LIGHTS FADE OUT. SOUND CUE: 8 BELLS TOLL.)

STEWARDESS: (*o.s.*) The Captain has posted the "fasten seat belts" sign, so if you'll make sure that your table trays are in an upright position—

(LIGHTS UP ON CENTER STAGE, as AIRPLANE PASSENGERS are back in original seats.)

CAPTAIN: (*o.s.*) —like to thank you for your patience...Flight 415 is now ready for takeoff—

(PASSENGERS cheer loudly; JENNIFER is staring at her GRANDMA)

JENNIFER: And that's the end of the story?

GRANDMA: That's the end of the story. And quite a story it was, don't you think?

(JENNIFER sits for a few moments with a thoughtful expression. Cries go up from the CHILDREN behind her, and the BUSINESSMAN and PROFESSOR across the aisle are arguing again.)

BUSINESSMAN: When are you pinko nitwits going to get it straight? You can't have your welfare cake and gum it down, too. You—

PROFESSOR: You've got a lotta nerve calling me—

(JENNIFER gets up and offers them each a stick of her neon-green licorice.)

BUSINESSMAN: What's this?

PROFESSOR: (*looks at JENNIFER through his bifocals*) It's some kind of girl.

BUSINESSMAN: What do you want? Are you selling something?

JENNIFER: It's licorice. Yummalicious Super-Zingy-Fresh-Chili-Pepper-Jelly flavor. Better than a breath mint.

PROFESSOR: For me?

JENNIFER: For both of you. Something to do with your mouth. Besides talking all the time.

(BUSINESSMAN and PROFESSOR take sticks, pop them into their mouths, smile.)

YOUNG MOTHER: Stephen! Stephen, stop it and settle down!

MICHAEL: Mommmmmmmm! My tummy hurts!

JENNIFER: Here. (*hands her stuffed dog to the MOTHER*) They might like to play with this.

MARIE: (*reaches out for toy*) Buppy bog! Buppy bog!

YOUNG MOTHER: Why, thank you! That's awfully kind. I'm sorry we're so cranky today. (*cuddles dog in CHILD'S arms*) It's just one of those cranky-wanky plane trips!

(JENNIFER speaks to GRANDMA.)

JENNIFER: What happened to Pieter? Did he ever get his own ship?

GRANDMA: A whole fleet of them. He got a big reward for helping save The Star of Copenhagen, and he put his money in savings while he went away to officer's school. Within ten years Pieter Zeeman had risen from cabin boy to one of the richest ship owners on the Atlantic route. And one of the very first to improve the safety and sailing conditions of his passenger ships.

JENNIFER: And Kitty? Did she and Pieter, like, go out and stuff once they got to Boston?

GRANDMA: (*chuckles*) Oh, she didn't stay long in Boston, oh no, not Grandma Kitty. She got employment as a private tutor with a family in Connecticut, helping their young children learn to read. Then when she was seventeen, she journeyed West across the frontier as a traveling schoolteacher. She must have taught in a hundred one-room school houses before she finally settled down in Omaha. Did you know she started the first public library system west of the Mississippi?

JENNIFER: Oh, bummer! I thought she and Pieter might have got married. That would be so totally romantic!

GRANDMA: Well, she *did* get married. You and I are living proof to that. And as for romance and adventure—well! That Kitty Doyle! *There* was a girl who wasn't afraid of *anything*.

JENNIFER: Not anything?

GRANDMA: Not a thing. Not even books.

(*JENNIFER smiles, picks up her homework book and begins reading. After a few moments, she looks up and gazes in front of her.*)

JENNIFER: (*dreamily*) Not afraid of anything. Wow, that sounds like a *real* life!

(*SOUND CUE: jet takeoff noises fade to sounds of a tinwhistle playing "The Bold Sailor Boy" and whispering ocean breezes billowing through tall white sails. LIGHTS FADE OUT.*)

THE END

The Bold Sailor Boy

(traditional, arranged by L.E. McCullough)

As I ro- ved out one ev- en- ing fair It
be- ing in the spring to take the night air I
spied a bold sai- lor and a la- dy so gay And I
stood near to lis- ten to what they would say

The Ship in Distress

(traditional, arranged by L.E. McCullough)

Twas two hun- dred mi- grant pil- grims cross- ing the white At- lan- tic
foam A- drift u- pon the ra- ging sea so far from hearth and
home The wea- ther proved to them hard cruel, their suff-'ring sad to
see With lives in trust to wick- ed men they sailed toward mi- se-
ry

The Parting Glass

(traditional, arranged by L.E. McCullough)

Oh, all the com- rades I ev- er had They're sor- ry for my

going a- way And all the sweet- hearts I ev- er knew They'd

wish me one more day to stay But since it falls u- pon my lot That

I should rise and you should not I gent- ly rise and soft- ly call "Good

night and joy be with you all"

ANNIE CHRISTMAS AND THE NATCHEZ TRACE BANDITS

Annie Christmas and the Natchez Trace Bandits is based upon a legendary ferry boat navigator and river roustabout named Annie Christmas, who flourished during the early 1800s along the Lower Mississippi, a stretch of river from Cairo to New Orleans also known as The Natchez Trace. Annie was reputed to have stood six feet eight inches in height, and it is entirely possible she had several encounters with river pirates such as the equally legendary Big Jim Girty. From the 1790s to the 1840s the Natchez Trace was one of the most dangerous stretches of territory in America, an area thick with thieves and cutthroats preying upon unwary travelers. Natchez Under the Hill was a notorious robbers' hideout located at the base of the bluff on which the city of Natchez was built; occasionally the gamblers and gunmen who infested the place shot at passing river boats for the fun of it. This story, in which the heroine uses her cleverness to outwit evildoers, incorporates several motifs from European *märchen* and American Jack tales.

TIME: The Present; 1822

PLACE: a nursing home in Natchez, Mississippi; a bandit's cave in Natchez Under the Hill

CAST: Annie Christmas   Mrs. Applegate
             Steamboat Willie   Julia
             Mrs. Ferguson   Big Jim Girty
             Sarah Ferguson   3 Bandits   Daniel Ferguson

STAGE SET: chair; boat; barrel; boulder; treasure pile; curtain; fire

PROPS: pistol; club; two Bowie knives; oar; cowhide; sack of corn kernels; jug; soup pot; soup bowl; spoon; napkin; tablecloth; sausage links; white flakes; whittling knife and stick

SPECIAL EFFECTS: pistol shots; corn popping; big splash

MUSIC: *Dance, Boatman, Dance; Turkey in the Straw; Little Brown Jug*

COSTUMES: Mrs. Applegate dresses in a business outfit with name tag over heart, Julia as a typical teen intern, Steamboat Willie in plaid shirt, trousers with suspenders and a railroader's cap; the Fergusons dress in formal early 19th-century clothes, bonnets for Sarah and her mother, knee breeches for Daniel; Big Jim Girty and his bandits wear frontier garb; Annie Christmas dresses in the work clothes of a standard river roustabout with a floppy hat, long leather hip boots, trousers, red or blue cotton shirt, black or brown waist jacket and a large belt sash

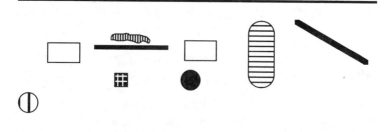

Stage Plan -- *Annie Christmas & the Natchez Trace Bandits*

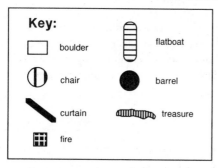

Key:

☐ boulder 🥚 flatboat

🎚 chair ● barrel

╲ curtain 〰 treasure

⊞ fire

(LIGHTS UP RIGHT. At stage right an old man, STEAMBOAT WILLIE, sits in a chair, whittling and humming. From right, MRS. APPLEGATE and JULIA enter and cross just to left of STEAMBOAT WILLIE, MRS. APPLEGATE talking as she fusses with her clothes and then JULIA'S clothes.)

MRS. APPLEGATE: My name is Mrs. Marjorie Applegate, recreation supervisor here at Hillcrest Manor. You may call me Mrs. Applegate. Now, Julia, as an entry-level intern, you'll begin your shift here in the parlor. *(looks around, perplexed)* It's usually quite full at this time of day. They can't all be at the doctor's. Or the mortician's. *(laughs idiotically)* Oh, excuse me, that's a nursing-home joke. Well, not to worry, you'll have plenty of opportunity to interact with—

STEAMBOAT WILLIE: *(shouts like a foghorn)* A-roooo000gh! A-roooo000gh!

MRS. APPLEGATE: *(startled)* Mr. Jenkins! *(strides to him)* Mr. Jenkins, how many times have I asked you to forbear from such outbursts?

(STEAMBOAT WILLIE sings chorus to "Dance, Boatman, Dance.")

STEAMBOAT WILLIE: *(sings)*
Heigh ho, boatman row, down the Mississippi from the Ohio
Heigh ho, boatman row, down the Mississippi from the Ohio

MRS. APPLEGATE: *(screeches)* Mr. Jenkins!

STEAMBOAT WILLIE: *(turns toward her as if he had been completely unaware of the womens' presence)* Oh, it's you again. The Memphis mailboat won't dock till quarter past three. You can wait by the cotton wharf yonder. It's shady there, and you might get a glimpse of the new *Belle of Baton Rouge* coming round the bend. They say she's a beaut!

MRS. APPLEGATE: Mr. Jenkins, I don't know if you remember me, but I am the recreation supervisor, Mrs.—

STEAMBOAT WILLIE: Course I remember who you are. I'm not stupid, just old. Mighty, mighty old.

MRS. APPLEGATE: *(to JULIA)* Mr. Jenkins is one of our more "spirited" residents.

STEAMBOAT WILLIE: Don't listen to a word she tells you, young lady. I'm *not* spirited. I'm crotchety, reckless and plumb loco as a panther pup what's got into a jar of eighty-proof white moonshine.

MRS. APPLEGATE: *(to JULIA in a loud whisper)* He thinks he was a riverboat captain.

STEAMBOAT WILLIE: And the name's Willie. Steamboat Willie. *(stands and bows, takes JULIA'S hand)*

JULIA: I'm pleased to meet you, Mr.—

MRS. APPLEGATE: Jenkins.

STEAMBOAT WILLIE: Steamboat Willie at your service, former pilot of the *Savannah Star*—my, what a glorious vessel! I've been on the river since I was knee high to a paddle wheel. Why, I'm so old, I knew Annie Christmas!

JULIA: Annie Christmas? Who's that?

MRS. APPLEGATE: Oh, don't get him started.

STEAMBOAT WILLIE: Who's Annie Christmas? A bright young Mississippi girl like you never heard of Annie Christmas?

JULIA: I'm awfully sorry, sir. Is it going to be on our SAT exam?

STEAMBOAT WILLIE: Well, you don't learn everything you need to know in life from schoolbooks. *(takes JULIA'S hand; he sits on chair and she sits on floor in front of him)* Here. Let me edificate you on some local history.

MRS. APPLEGATE: I'll see you after lunch, Julia…if I can hold mine. *(exits right, huffily)*

(LIGHTS UP LEFT on ANNIE CHRISTMAS and her three passengers—youngsters SARAH FERGUSON and DANIEL FERGUSON and their mother, MRS. FERGUSON; ANNIE rows the flatboat, the FERGUSONS sit behind and beside her, MRS. FERGUSON prim and proper, SARAH and DANIEL nudging each other and pointing at the shore. MUSIC: fiddle plays "Dance, Boatman, Dance" under dialogue.)

STEAMBOAT WILLIE: Back away back, when most Americans traveled by water, Annie Christmas was the Queen of the Mississippi River ferry runners. She'd run folks up and down the river, from one side to the other, in no time at all. Did you say she was fast? Child, Annie Christmas was so fast, it took three people to see her when she ran: one to say, "Here she comes!", another to say, "Here she is!", and a third to say, "There she goes!" And tall! She was so tall that when it rained, she got wet fifteen minutes before anybody else. She was so nimble she could stand a ladder straight up and down, then climb to the top rung, pull it up after her, then climb up again. In fact, she was married to a man whose feet were so big he had to put his pants on by pulling them over his head, but that's another story for another time. *This* story is about the night she met the worst bandit in the whole Natchez Trace.

(LIGHTS OUT on STEAMBOAT WILLIE and JULIA; MUSIC is up for a few seconds, then fades out as ANNIE stops rowing and peers around intently.)

MRS. FERGUSON: *(to ANNIE)* Madam! Madam! Why are we stopped here? And where are we? I can't see a thing in this fetid darkness!

(ANNIE does not reply, but puts her head down low as if listening to something under the water.)

MRS. FERGUSON: I say, this is an outrage!

SARAH FERGUSON: Mother, please. She's listening.

MRS. FERGUSON: I *know* what she's doing, Sarah. She's stopped rowing, and we are in serious danger of missing our connecting boat in Natchez. Oh, this is an outrage! Madam, I say, madam!

DANIEL FERGUSON: Her name is Annie, mother. Annie Christmas. Like the holiday.

MRS. FERGUSON: Daniel Ferguson, I am well aware of her name. It's her increasingly eccentric behavior that has me—ohhhh!

(MRS. FERGUSON tumbles backward as ANNIE straightens and begins rowing furiously; DANIEL moves up and stands on ANNIE'S right.)

DANIEL FERGUSON: Annie, what is it? River pirates?

(SARAH FERGUSON moves up and stands on ANNIE'S left.)

SARAH FERGUSON: Miss Christmas, when I told my friends back in Boston we were going to travel down the Mississippi River to New Orleans, they said we'd never make it through the Natchez Trace. They said it was a hundred miles of nothing but cutthroats and evildoers—

DANIEL FERGUSON: Scalawags and renegades!

SARAH FERGUSON: Savages and villains!

DANIEL FERGUSON: Lowdown, good-for-nothing, back-stabbing ruffians and bushwhackers!

MRS. FERGUSON: *(stands up)* Such language! I will not permit—ohhhh!

(ANNIE abruptly stops rowing and MRS. FERGUSON tumbles back.)

ANNIE CHRISTMAS: You folks are right to be a touch troubled. This is Big Jim Girty's territory, from here to Red Bluff.

DANIEL FERGUSON: Big Jim Girty? Who is he, Annie?

ANNIE CHRISTMAS: Just past that bend is the town of Natchez. If it was daylight, you'd see it shining bright and silvery on the cliffs—the prettiest settlement on the river, for my money. But below those cliffs is another Natchez . . .

SARAH FERGUSON: Another Natchez?

ANNIE CHRISTMAS: They call it "Natchez Under the Hill," and it's filled to the chock brim with the rankest scoundrels in the whole of

Creation. They meet there and divvy up their loot, fiddling and dancing till the break of day.

DANIEL FERGUSON: Sounds exciting.

MRS. FERGUSON: Daniel!

DANIEL FERGUSON: But thoroughly wicked.

ANNIE CHRISTMAS: There are a hundred bandit chiefs in Natchez Under the Hill. And Big Jim Girty is the worst one of all.

DANIEL FERGUSON: *(gleefully)* Bully!

SARAH FERGUSON: Daniel! Ssssshhhhh!

(ANNIE resumes rowing slowly; a few seconds later a pistol shot rings out and three BANDITS step from behind left curtain and stand to the left side of the boat, BANDIT #1 brandishing a pistol, BANDIT #2 a club, BANDIT #3 a long Bowie knife.)

BANDIT #1: Hold fast, pilgrims! Or I'll keelhaul the lot of ye!

(THE FERGUSONS recoil in alarm; BANDITS #2 and #3 hop aboard to take control of boat.)

SARAH FERGUSON: Bandits!

MRS. FERGUSON: Ohhhh! We're surrounded!

(ANNIE picks up an oar and smacks BANDIT #2; he falls into BANDIT #3 and both tumble into water; BANDIT #1 fires a shot in the air and points pistol at ANNIE.)

BANDIT #1: One more swing of that toothpick, mademoiselle, and you'll be swimmin' with the gators. Step ashore now, nice and easy.

ANNIE CHRISTMAS: *(to the FERGUSONS)* Do as he says.

(THE FERGUSONS step ashore, followed by ANNIE; they are hustled to center stage—BIG JIM GIRTY'S lair in Natchez Under the Hill.)

DANIEL FERGUSON: This is a really deep cave!

SARAH FERGUSON: It's frightful!

DANIEL FERGUSON: It's bully!

MRS. FERGUSON: Daniel!

(THE BANDITS herd ANNIE and the FERGUSONS before a large boulder, BANDIT #1 taps the boulder with his pistol three times.)

BANDIT #1: Well, I had an old hen and she had a wooden leg.

BANDIT #2: Just the best old hen that ever laid an egg.

BANDIT #3: She laid more eggs than any chicken on the farm.

(BIG JIM GIRTY steps from behind the boulder)

BIG JIM GIRTY: And another little sip wouldn't do her no harm. Hello, boys! Well, you brought some fresh chickens tonight. They look rich and ready for pluckin'!

MRS. FERGUSON: *(steps forward)* Sir, are you the leader of this rapscallion band?

BIG JIM GIRTY: No, ma'am, I'm the mother superior from St. Bernadette's! *(he and BANDITS guffaw)*

MRS. FERGUSON: I *demand* we be released at once. *I* am Flora Ferguson of the Massachusetts Fergusons. My late husband was a brigadier general in the War of 1812. My father was a member of the Continental Congress, and my brother Nathan is President Monroe's special envoy to Belgium.

BIG JIM GIRTY: Well, I'll be switched with a monkey's tailfeathers. We've hauled in a catch of bluebloods tonight, boys. They'll bring a pretty penny in ransom. *(approaches ANNIE)* And, who's our winsome ferry lass?

DANIEL FERGUSON: She's Annie Christmas, and she's the best flatboater on the Mississippi! You should have seen her knock those two plankers off their feet with one swipe!

MRS. FERGUSON: Daniel!

DANIEL FERGUSON: It was bully!

SARAH & MRS. FERGUSON: Daniel! *(they pull him back)*

BIG JIM GIRTY: *(scrutinizes her closely)* I've heard of you, Annie Christmas. They say you're a legend on the river, from Minnesota to the Gulf of Mexico.

ANNIE CHRISTMAS: I don't set much stock in loose words. I prefer action.

BIG JIM GIRTY: A woman after my own heart. What sort of action do you prefer?

ANNIE CHRISTMAS: Folks talk about you, too, Big Jim Girty. They say you've got a storehouse of treasure hidden away…an acre of ill-gotten gains. Do you really? Or is it just talk?

BIG JIM GIRTY: *(laughs)* Ha-ha-ha! When they say Big Jim Girty is the richest bandit in the Natchez Trace, it ain't just talk.

ANNIE CHRISTMAS: Prove it.

(BIG JIM GIRTY hesitates a moment, then crosses up right and pulls aside a ragged curtain revealing a huge pile of treasure; THE FERGU-SONS gasp.)

SARAH FERGUSON: Like Ali Baba and the Forty Thieves!

BANDIT #1: Hold your tongue, girlie!

BANDIT #2: We didn't steal none of this. People just give it to us outa gratitude.

BANDIT #3: For not killin' 'em. Haw-haw-haw! *(guffaws, BANDITS #1 and #2 snicker)*

BIG JIM GIRTY: *(takes a 12"x 12" piece of cowhide and hands it to ANNIE)* Here you go, mademoiselle. To show how generous I am, you can have as much treasure as this cowhide can cover.

ANNIE CHRISTMAS: This one little piece of cowhide? That *is* very generous, monsieur. *(grabs knife from belt of BANDIT #3)* If I may borrow this pour une momente…merci beaucoups.

(She lays cowhide on the ground and, starting from the center, cuts it into several thin strips that she lays out in a perimeter, covering a huge area.)

ANNIE CHRISTMAS: That's how much treasure this cowhide can cover!

(FERGUSONS titter; BANDITS grumble, BANDIT #3 grabs back his knife.)

BIG JIM GIRTY: *(throws down his hat and stomps it)* Oooohhhh! You outsmarted me, woman. And I *hate* that. Now, I'm just gonna have to go out and rob some more! You're a-makin' me do it!

BANDIT #2: Can we come with you, Big Jim?

BIG JIM GIRTY: Are you out of you skulls! If you come with me, who's gonna guard the prisoners?

(BANDITS point to each other.)

BANDITS #1, #2, #3: He will!

BIG JIM GIRTY: Morons! *You* captured these pilgrims, and *you'll* guard 'em! *I'm* gonna do the robbin'! *(BANDITS grumble)* You be on your toes with this one here, this Annie Christmas. She's a tricky lass, right enough. *(he walks to ANNIE, who turns away)* If we'd met under more favorable circumstances, I might have considered takin' you under my wing, so to speak. *(BANDITS snicker)*

ANNIE CHRISTMAS: The only wings you'll ever see are angel wings, Big Jim Girty. And you'll see them from the hot place down below.

BIG JIM GIRTY: *(glowers, shakes his fist)* Guard 'em! *(exits left, stomping)*

BANDIT #1: Good, he's gone. Now we can get social! *(shouts to offstage)* Hey there, fiddler! Strike up a tune!

(MUSIC fades up: "Turkey in the Straw" played by fiddle; BANDITS #1, #2 and #3 clog dance and sing.)

BANDIT #1: *(sings)*
Well, I hitched up the wagon and I drove it down the road
With a two-horse wagon and a four-horse load

BANDIT #2: *(sings)*
"Crack!" went the whip, and the lead horse sprung
And I said goodbye to the wagon tongue

BANDIT #3: *(sings)*
Turkey in the hay!

BANDITS #1 & #2: *(sing)*
Hay-hay-hay!

BANDIT #3: *(sings)*
Turkey in the straw!

BANDITS #1 & #2: *(sing)*
Haw-haw-haw!

BANDIT #3: *(sings)*
Pick em up, shake em up, anyway at all

BANDITS #1, #2 & #3: *(sing)*
And strike up a tune called "Turkey in the Straw"

(MUSIC ends; BANDITS laugh, hoot, holler, playfully punch each other before noticing their captives.)

BANDIT #2: *(to BANDIT #1)* Come on, let's go find a poker game. We'll get back before Big Jim.

BANDIT #1: *(hands his pistol to BANDIT #3)* Take this, and watch 'em close. *(BANDITS #1 and #2 exit left as BANDIT #3 settles back against barrel)*

SARAH FERGUSON: *(loud whisper)* Annie, I'm frightened. If these men don't get a ransom, would they kill us?

ANNIE CHRISTMAS: Most likely.

MRS. FERGUSON: They can't do that; we'd miss our boat to New Orleans!

DANIEL FERGUSON: What are we going to do?

ANNIE CHRISTMAS: Tell a tale or two, I reckon.

BANDIT #3: *(yawns)* Dang, I'm tired. You're about the thirteenth boatload of travelers we ambushed since Sunday. *(brandishes pistol)* But don't get any silly ideas about escapin', or I'll blast you to Kingdom Come!

MRS. FERGUSON: Utter blasphemy!

ANNIE CHRISTMAS: We wouldn't think of getting any ideas like that, would we, folks?

DANIEL & SARAH FERGUSON: Oh no, no…not at all, no, never.

ANNIE CHRISTMAS: In fact, we'll all just sit down and get real comfortable and help you stand guard. *(motions for FERGUSONS to sit)* Daniel, go fetch up another log for the fire. Sarah, bring the man that nice wool blanket.

BANDIT #3: That's right kind of you, Annie Christmas.

ANNIE CHRISTMAS: *(curtseys)* I was raised poor but proper. *(sits and draws her jacket around her)* My, there's a chill coming off the river tonight, isn't there?

DANIEL & SARAH FERGUSON: Oh yes, yes…a chill, very cold, freezing, brrrrr.

(BANDIT #3 snuggles deeper into his cloak and blanket.)

ANNIE CHRISTMAS: Why, it reminds me of a night in Kentucky some time ago, near Paducah. Just after midnight there came a tremendous storm whistling down from the prairie. Why, it blew the feathers off a chicken and chipmunks out of their holes. It forced birds to fly backwards to keep sand out of their eyes. It saved a rabbit's life— when a fox came after him, the rabbit put up his ears, and they caught the wind like a pair of sails and carried him clean away.

(FERGUSONS, BANDIT laugh)

ANNIE CHRISTMAS: The wind of this storm was so powerful, it blew the cracks out of a fence, the teeth out of a saw and a well out of the ground. It moved a county line, changed the time of day and the day of the week and kept the sun setting for a whole day until it could catch up with itself and come back before the morning after.

(FERGUSONS chuckle; BANDIT starts to nod; ANNIE rises slowly and walks around the drowsing BANDIT)

ANNIE CHRISTMAS: This wind blew the hair off a man's head, the whiskers off his face, the shoes off his socks, the socks off his feet, the toenails off his toes. And when he opened his mouth, he swallowed ten barrels of air that blew him up to ten times his normal size and sent him bouncing all across the state like a giant bubble till he blew into Tennessee and got blown against a stone wall…which flattened him thin as a piece of paper that got found and peeled off by a circuit-riding preacher and used as posters for his next holiness revival. *(she peeks at the snoring BANDIT)*

SARAH FERGUSON: *(loud whisper)* I think he's asleep, Annie!

ANNIE CHRISTMAS: Daniel, fetch me up that sack of corn kernels. Now, throw it on the fire. All of it.

(SOUND: popcorn popping in a crackling fire.)

DANIEL FERGUSON: Gadzooks, will you look at that? It's turning into flakes!

SARAH FERGUSON: Big white flakes all over the ground! Like snow!

ANNIE CHRISTMAS: Gather up the flakes and spread them around our friend. Big heaps of flakes! Just like winter!

(DANIEL and SARAH spread huge mounds of popped corn around BANDIT #3, then join ANNIE and MRS. FERGUSON behind the boulder as BANDIT #3 awakes.)

BANDIT #3: Jumpin' jehosophat! It's one of those blue northers Annie Christmas talked about! *(sits up, shivering)* Why, it's snowed a foot in the cave! Probably ten feet outside! I'm snowed in! It's freezing! I'll never make it out! I'm…I'm…I'm freezing to death. *(shivers, expires)*

(THE FERGUSONS and ANNIE watch him as he stiffens, then come out and gather around his corpse.)

SARAH FERGUSON: He froze himself to death!

ANNIE CHRISTMAS: Just like most snakes: too cold-blooded for their own good. Daniel, hand me that sack and follow me out to the cave entrance.

(ANNIE and DANIEL cross to down center, where ANNIE crawls into the sack.)

DANIEL FERGUSON: Annie! What are you doing?

ANNIE CHRISTMAS: Tie the top. Now, get back inside. Hurry!

(DANIEL ties the top, then scurries back to his SISTER and MOTHER. A few seconds later, BANDIT #2 enters from left, singing "Little Brown Jug" and sipping from a liquor jug.)

BANDIT #2:

Ha-ha-ha, ho-ho-he; little brown jug don't I love thee

Ha-ha-ha, you and me; little brown jug yes I love thee

(He sees the sack, cautiously walks around it and jumps back when it moves.)

BANDIT #2: Whaaa!

ANNIE CHRISTMAS: *(moans)* Ohhhhhh…help me…somebody help me and get a rich reward.

BANDIT #2: *(pokes the sack with his jug)* What are you doin' in there? *(hiccups)*

ANNIE CHRISTMAS: The governor put me in here.

BANDIT #2: The governor? What for?

ANNIE CHRISTMAS: Cause I'm a poor speller.

BANDIT #2: Poor speller? Since when is bein' a poor speller a crime in Mississippi? *(hiccups)*

ANNIE CHRISTMAS: Since the governor said so. I captured a desperate bandit last month, and the governor wanted to give me a big reward and a big fancy dress ball. But when they found out I couldn't spell right, they told me I had to stay here in this sack. But if somebody comes along and can spell the word, then they can have the reward and fancy ball.

BANDIT #2: Is that so? Big reward, eh? Tell me, what was you supposed to spell?

ANNIE CHRISTMAS: "Idiot."

BANDIT #2: What'd you call me? *(hiccups)*

ANNIE CHRISTMAS: "Idiot". The word I was supposed to spell was "idiot."

BANDIT #2: Idiot? *(laughs)* Shucks, everybody knows how to spell idiot. E-d-e...uh, lessee...e-u-t. E-dee-ut.

ANNIE CHRISTMAS: That's it! You can get the reward!

BANDIT #2: What do I do? What do I do?

ANNIE CHRISTMAS: Untie this sack and get in. I'll take you to the governor's mansion, and when they ask you how to spell "idiot," you spell it and get the reward.

(BANDIT unties sack; ANNIE gets out and helps BANDIT inside.)

BANDIT #2: You know, you look kinda familiar. *(hiccups)*

ANNIE CHRISTMAS: *(she takes the jug from him)* Everybody looks familiar when you look through one of these. Better get in if you want that special reward.

(He ducks inside the sack, which she ties tight.)

ANNIE CHRISTMAS: Here we go!

BANDIT #2: I'm primed and ready!

ANNIE CHRISTMAS: Darn-tootin'!

(She rolls him to stage left and dumps him in the river—rolls him off-stage. SOUND: big splash.)

ANNIE CHRISTMAS: *(shouts after him)* Governor's mansion is downstream about forty miles. With a good current you'll be there by June.

(She dusts her hands and returns to the cave; BANDIT #1 enters from left and slowly moves across stage to cave.)

DANIEL FERGUSON: What happened to that bandit you were talking to?

ANNIE CHRISTMAS: He took a notion to have a bath. *(sees BANDIT #1 coming)* Huzzah! Looks like we've got more company coming. Gather round...

(She gathers THE FERGUSONS into a huddle, and they whisper together until BANDIT #1 enters.)

BANDIT #1: *(points to BANDIT #3)* What happened to him?

SARAH FERGUSON: He fell asleep and dreamed he was in a snowstorm.

BANDIT #1: *(kneels and feels dead BANDIT'S face)* Why, he's a dadgum icicle! Say, what kind of shenanigans is goin' on here? Where's his pistol at?

ANNIE CHRISTMAS: Right here, monsieur. *(hands pistol to him)* You have nothing to fear from us. We are honest prisoners.

BANDIT #1: *(chuckles)* Honest. And *crazy.*

MRS. FERGUSON: We're just polite. In fact, we were about to discuss preparations for supper. Dear sir bandit, would you care to join us for a bite?

BANDIT #1: Tarnation, I've got a powerful hunger upon me wrasslin' me down like a grizzly bear! You folks got any good grub?

MRS. FERGUSON: Unfortunately, no. We have nothing to eat at all.

SARAH FERGUSON: Mother, I know how to make boot soup.

BANDIT #1: Boot soup? What's that?

DANIEL FERGUSON: It's delicious! We eat it in Boston all the time.

SARAH FERGUSON: It goes wonderfully with baked scrod and lima beans.

BANDIT #1: *(grimaces, rubs his stomach)* Well, I wouldn't mind having a bowl or two now, boot soup or no.

ANNIE CHRISTMAS: We can use my boots. They'll give the most broth. Stoke up the fire, Daniel.

MRS. FERGUSON: And sir bandit, you just relax and enjoy your meal. *(calls out offstage)* Mr. Fiddler, some dining music, if you please!

(MUSIC UP: "Turkey in the Straw" played by fiddle. ANNIE takes off her long hip boots and puts them in the soup pot. BANDIT sits and relaxes as SARAH and MRS. FERGUSON wait on him, setting a tablecloth on the barrel, tucking a napkin in his shirt, etc. while ANNIE stirs the soup. MUSIC FADES OUT after a verse; ANNIE dishes up a bowl of boot soup and serves it to the BANDIT.)

BANDIT #1: Why, thank you, Annie. *(smells soup)* Mmmm-mmm. Sure smells tasty! *(begins guzzling soup)*

ANNIE CHRISTMAS: It *is* tasty, monsieur. Because of the special ingredients.

BANDIT #1: Special ingredients? *(guzzles soup)*

ANNIE CHRISTMAS: It's all in the seasoning. Every day working along the river, about thirty water moccasins and copperheads sink their fangs into those boots. After a few years, that's a lot of stored-up snake venom stirring around in that leather.

SARAH FERGUSON: And when you boil the leather—

MRS. FERGUSON: It adds just the right amount of flavor—poison!

BANDIT #1: *(guzzles soup)* Tarnation, this is deeee-licious! *(picks up bowl and drains it)* I do declare, Annie Christmas, your boot soup is to die for!

(BANDIT stiffens, drops bowl, collapses dead.)

ANNIE CHRISTMAS: I disdain a flatterer. Move him.

(THE FERGUSONS move BANDIT #1 next to BANDIT #3; BIG JIM GIRTY enters from left.)

BIG JIM GIRTY: My men! *(rushes to them, verifies they are deceased)* How did this happen?

DANIEL FERGUSON: *(points)* That one froze to death.

SARAH FERGUSON: *(points)* That one had a bad stomach ache.

MRS. FERGUSON: And there's one went swimming with the alligators. He hasn't returned.

BIG JIM GIRTY: *(strides angrily to ANNIE)* Are you a sorceress?

ANNIE CHRISTMAS: Let's just say I have a vivid imagination. Which is more than I can say for you, "Little Jim."

BIG JIM GIRTY: What'd you call me?

ANNIE CHRISTMAS: I called you a weak, sniveling coward. A pathetic braggart and mange-ridden spawn of a beggar's cur.

BIG JIM GIRTY: How dare you!

ANNIE CHRISTMAS: Are you man enough to challenge me to a duel?

BIG JIM GIRTY: A duel? With you? *(laughs)* Hardly!

ANNIE CHRISTMAS: So you are not a man, but a mouse?

BIG JIM GIRTY: I do not lower myself to duel with a woman.

ANNIE CHRISTMAS: Squeak-squeak-squeak…hear the little mousie go squeak-squeak-squeak…

BIG JIM GIRTY: That is enough, mademoiselle!

ANNIE CHRISTMAS: Squeak-squeak-squeak…hear the little mousie go squeak-squeak-squeak…

BIG JIM GIRTY: I must warn you…you are provoking me!

ANNIE CHRISTMAS & THE FERGUSONS: Squeak-squeak-squeak …hear the little mousie go squeak-squeak-squeak…

BIG JIM GIRTY: *(puts hands over his ears)* I am not listening, I am not listening to you.

ANNIE CHRISTMAS & THE FERGUSONS: Squeak-squeak-squeak …hear the little mousie go squeak-squeak-squeak…

BIG JIM GIRTY: All right! All right! I challenge you to a duel, Annie Christmas!

ANNIE CHRISTMAS: I accept. Now, I choose the weapons. Bowie knives.

BIG JIM GIRTY: Bowie knives it is! Prepare to meet your doom, Annie Christmas!

(They draw knives and square off; ANNIE stops and straightens.)

ANNIE CHRISTMAS: Une momente, monsieur…

BIG JIM GIRTY: What is it?

ANNIE CHRISTMAS: I am not dressed for the occasion.

BIG JIM GIRTY: Not dressed?

MRS. FERGUSON: Surely you wouldn't expect a woman to engage in a deadly duel-to-the-death dressed like *that?*

BIG JIM GIRTY: I wouldn't know, ma'am. I ain't no dadblasted, per-fume-drippin', skirt-totin' woman!

MRS. FERGUSON: Give us a minute, sir.

(She takes ANNIE aside and begins fussing with her hair, then stops and addresses GIRTY.)

MRS. FERGUSON: Would you mind turning around? Barbarian!

(Exasperated, GIRTY turns around, grumbling and tapping his foot impatiently as SARAH stuffs a large string of sausage links into a sash around ANNIE'S waist and MRS. FERGUSON puts up ANNIE'S hair.)

BIG JIM GIRTY: Are you ready?

MRS. FERGUSON: She's ready! Oh, you look so elegant with your hair above your ears.

(GIRTY turns around and squares off; ANNIE stops and straightens.)

BIG JIM GIRTY: Great flippin' catfish, what is it now?

ANNIE CHRISTMAS: This is a waste of time. I refuse to fight a man who is a weakling.

BIG JIM GIRTY: Weakling? I'm no weakling! I'm Big Jim Girty, the wickedest bandit in the Natchez Trace! I'm tough as nails, rugged as rawhide and meaner than a panther with a ten-year toothache! I'm a depraved killer of men, women and helpless water fowl. I can out-spit, out-scream, out-wrestle any five Mississippians or fifteen normal humans. I'm Big Jim Girty, and I am *baaaaaaad!*

ANNIE CHRISTMAS: You're a milksop!

(She plunges her knife into her belt sash, ripping it open; sausages spill out and FERGUSONS gasp as ANNIE grimaces, staggers, then rights herself.)

BIG JIM GIRTY: Good lord, woman, I never seen so many guts come out of one belly!

ANNIE CHRISTMAS: I'd like to see you try that.

BIG JIM GIRTY: You bet your mittens!

(He takes his knife and plunges it into his stomach, grimaces, staggers, falls to his knees and dies dramatically.)

ANNIE CHRISTMAS: There are some things about a woman a man will never understand.

(THE FERGUSONS cheer and crowd around her; they gather up armloads of treasure and exit left. LIGHTS UP RIGHT on STEAMBOAT WILLIE and JULIA.)

STEAMBOAT WILLIE: And that's how Annie Christmas won a treasure, saved her passengers and killed the worst bandit in the Natchez Trace.

(He turns away and resumes whittling, humming "Turkey in the Straw"; JULIA rises and crosses to MRS. APPLEGATE who has entered from left and stands at center, impatiently looking at her watch.)

JULIA: Mrs. Applegate! Did you hear that? That was an incredible story!

MRS. APPLEGATE: They always are.

JULIA: Do you…do you think any of what Steamboat Willie—I mean, Mr. Jenkins—said…really happened?

MRS. APPLEGATE: Young lady, when you've worked here as long as I have, you'll be able to answer that for yourself. Now, if you're quite finished listening to fairy tales and fal-de-rol, you can follow me to the linen room.

JULIA: Yes, Mrs. Applegate.

(MRS. APPLEGATE exits left, briskly. JULIA starts to follow, but stops and turns to look at STEAMBOAT WILLIE; making sure MRS. APPLEGATE has gone, JULIA tiptoes back to him.)

JULIA: Mr. Willie?

STEAMBOAT WILLIE: Yes, my dear?

JULIA: Did Annie Christmas ever have any children?

STEAMBOAT WILLIE: *(stops whittling and turns to her)* Funny you should say that, because she did, you know. In fact, the daughter looked a lot like you.

(JULIA sits back down at his feet as he begins telling another story. LIGHTS FADE OUT.)

STEAMBOAT WILLIE: I had a picture of her once. Oh, she was pretty as a Georgia peach in the month of September. And strong? Why, they say she was even stronger than her mother. Isabella was her name…

(MUSIC UP: "Dance, Boatman, Dance" sung by chorus offstage—3 BANDITS, 3 FERGUSONS)

CHORUS: *(sings)*

Boatman dance, boatman sing, boatman do most anything
Boatman dance, boatman sing, boatman do most anything

Dance, boatman, dance; dance, boatman, dance
Dance all night to the broad daylight and go home with the gals in
the morning

Heigh ho, boatman row, down the Mississippi from the Ohio
Heigh ho, boatman row, down the Mississippi from the Ohio

Dance, boatman, dance; dance, boatman, dance
Dance all night to the broad daylight and go home with the gals in
the morning

THE END

Dance, Boatman, Dance
(written by Dan Emmet, arranged by L.E. McCullough)

Boat-man dance, boat-man sing, boat-man do most a- ny- thing

Dance, boat-man, dance; dance, boat- man, dance; Dance all night to the

broad day- light and go home with the gals in the mor- ning

Heigh ho, boat-man row, down the Miss-is- sip-pi from the O- hi- o

Heigh ho, boat-man row, down the Miss-is- sip- pi from the O- hi- o

Little Brown Jug
(traditional, arranged by L.E. McCullough)

Ha- ha- ha, ho- ho- he; lit- tle brown jug, don't I love thee?

Ha- ha- ha, you and me; lit- tle brown jug, yes I love thee!

Turkey in the Straw
(traditional, arranged by L.E. McCullough)

Well, I hitched up the wa- gon and I drove it down the road with a

two- horse wa- gon and a four- horse load "Crack!" went the whip, and the

lead horse sprung And I said good- bye to the wa- gon tongue

Tur- key in the hay! Hay- hay- hay! Tur- key in the straw!

Haw- haw- haw! Pick 'em up, shake 'em up, a- ny- way at all And

strike up a tune called "Tur- key in the Straw"

"YOU'RE LIVE WITH BIG-FOOT WALLACE!"

Have you ever wondered what happens to old myths and legends in modern times? The best of them don't fade away but are reshaped to suit the purposes of today's world. Why, they've even been known to show up in person and spin their ageless yarns for new generations of eager listeners in some of the most peculiar places...

TIME: Live at Five!

PLACE: Daytime Television, USA

CAST:
John Henry	Big-Foot Wallace
Joe Magarac	White Painted Woman
Old Stormalong	Ma-aui
Sandy Starr	Marty Million
Announcer	4 Audience Members
Caller	

STAGE SET: television studio interior—6 guests sitting at center stage, 4 audience members at down right, a sign hanging above center stage reading *America Blabs!*

PROPS: 6 lavalier microphones for Tall Tales; 2 hand-held microphones for Co-hosts; placards reading: *Applause; Boo-Hiss; Cut to Commercial; 30 Sec.*

SPECIAL EFFECTS: sound—canned applause audio track

COSTUMES: Sandy and Marty wear standard talk show host suits with appropriate plastic-pouf hairstyles; audience dress in everyday leisure clothes; Tall Tale characters appear as their typical legendary representation—White Painted Woman wears traditional Apache dress and carries a hand drum; Ma-aui wears a loin cloth and a seashell necklace and is covered with tattoos, a knife hanging from his waist; Old Stormalong is in 19th-century sea captain outfit with a smoking pipe; John Henry wears railroad overalls and carries two hammers; Big-Foot Wallace is a Texas Ranger with six-gun and holster; Joe Magarac wears steel-worker outfit of coveralls and a plate of shiny silver that appears when he exposes his chest

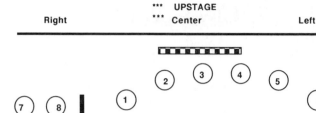

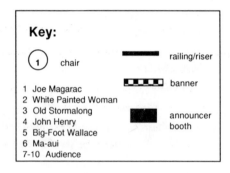

Stage Plan -- *"You're Live with Big-Foot Wallace!"*

Key:

(1) chair

■■■■■■■ railing/riser

◻◼◻◼◻◼◻ banner

■■■■ announcer booth

1 Joe Magarac
2 White Painted Woman
3 Old Stormalong
4 John Henry
5 Big-Foot Wallace
6 Ma-aui
7-10 Audience

(STAGE DARK. SOUND: CANNED AUDIENCE APPLAUSE.)

ANNOUNCER: *(o.s.)* Helllllllllllllllll-o, America! It's time for your favorite daily talkathon, *America Blabs!*, with your relentlessly perky co-hosts Sandy Starr—

(SPOTLIGHT ON SANDY STARR ENTERING FROM STAGE LEFT.)

ANNOUNCER: *(o.s.):* And Marty Million!

(SPOTLIGHT ON MARTY MILLION ENTERING FROM STAGE RIGHT. Applause continues as SANDY and MARTY skip to center stage, shake hands, hug, kiss each other's cheek twice, giggle, nudge each other, bounce up and down idiotically and finally face auditorium; applause stops immediately. LIGHTS UP FULL)

SANDY: Hi, Marty!

MARTY: Hi, Sandy!

SANDY & MARTY: And, helllllllllllllll-o, America!

SANDY: We sure hope you're ready to blab!

MARTY: And pay close attention to each one of our sponsors' mindless commercials.

SANDY: Marty, we have an absolutely exciting bunch of guests with us. Guess what today's topic is.

MARTY: Dead sunburn skin and how to recycle it?

SANDY: No!

MARTY: Serial turtle killers who have sex with their cufflinks, and the lawyers who love them?

SANDY: Oh, you wild and crazy guy! Today's topic is—"America's Tall Tales: Where Are They Now?"

(ANNOUNCER holds up "Applause" sign; AUDIENCE applauds.)

MARTY: Boy, does that sound like a wei-ner! Yuk-yuk-yuk! *(laughs stupidly; applause stops)*

SANDY: And we've been asked by our producers to warn you viewers at home, as well as those in our live studio audience, that the incredible feats of magic and superhuman physical prowess you may witness on today's show should not be attempted without the assistance of a certified professional.

MARTY: Is that guy with the blue ox coming? You know, the lumberjack that eats Montana for breakfast?

SANDY: Paul Bunyan?

MARTY: No, your fiancé! Yuk-yuk-yuk! *(laughs stupidly)*

(ANNOUNCER holds up "Applause" sign; AUDIENCE applauds briefly, stops when ANNOUNCER drops sign.)

SANDY: Let's introduce our guests. Who do we have with us today, Marty?

MARTY: From Pittsburgh, P.A., we have Joe Magarac, the nation's own mighty Man of Steel!

(JOE MAGARAC enters, bows, takes seat on dais; ANNOUNCER holds up "Applause" sign; AUDIENCE applauds.)

MARTY: And from the Wild, Wild West in the land of way too much turquoise jewelry, it's White Painted Woman, Mother of All Apache!

(WHITE PAINTED WOMAN enters, bows, takes seat on dais; AN-NOUNCER holds up "Applause" sign; AUDIENCE applauds.)

MARTY: Then, a crusty old son of the salty sea, it's Barnacle Bill's first cousin, Old Stormalong!

(OLD STORMALONG enters, bows, takes seat on dais; ANNOUNCER holds up "Applause" sign; AUDIENCE applauds.)

MARTY: And the Man with the Hammer, that Railroad Tie Whammer, Jammin' Johhhhhhn Henry!

(JOHN HENRY enters, bows, takes seat on dais; ANNOUNCER holds up "Applause" sign; AUDIENCE applauds.)

MARTY: From the Lone Star state of Texas—aw, c'mon, people, surely they've got more than one diddly-doodle star in the whole state of Texas!—it's Mr. Law 'n' Order West of the Pecos himself, Big-Foot Wallace!

(BIG-FOOT WALLACE enters, bows, takes seat on dais; ANNOUNCER holds up "Applause" sign; AUDIENCE applauds.)

MARTY: And, last but not least, straight from the land of luaus and hula hoops, a man who never met a tattoo he didn't like, Ma-aui!

(MA-AUI enters, bows, takes seat on dais; ANNOUNCER holds up "Applause" sign; AUDIENCE applauds.)

SANDY: What a super bunch of guests! Welcome to *America Blabs!*, everyone. Let's do ladies first, shall we? White Painted Woman, you're known as Mother of All Apache. Is that because of your long-standing interest in child welfare issues?

WHITE PAINTED WOMAN: *(slowly, with dignity)* I am Mother of all Apache. I have existed for all time, from the beginning of all time, before there was time. I gave thunder and lightning, rain and sun, stars and moon, plants and animals to the people. I gave people power over animals, over darkness, over disease and death. Today, when Apache girls become women in the Sunrise Dance, they sing to me: *(stands and chants, beating her drum)*
White Painted Woman commands that which lies above
White Painted Woman's power emerges
White Painted Woman carries this girl

She carries her through long life
She carries her to good fortune
She carries her to old age
She carries her to peaceful sleep

(WHITE PAINTED WOMAN sits; no one reacts for several seconds, then ANNOUNCER holds up "Applause" sign; AUDIENCE applauds.)

MARTY: That's just amazing, isn't it, audience? A real family values story there. And now from the beautiful islands of blue Hawaii, let's hear from Ma-aui. Ma-aui, dude—*incredible* tattoos! You and Axl Rose should get together and compare notes. Yuk-yuk-yuk! Get it, notes! *Musical* notes, Axl Rose is a musician! Yuk-yuk-yuk! *(laughs stupidly, AUDIENCE titters)*

MA-AUI: *(stands, waves arm and gains immediate silence; points to his tattoos as he speaks)* These are the great deeds of Ma-aui, creator of the universe. Ma-aui, who lifted up the sky to where it is now, above the trees and the mountains. Ma-aui, who brought birds to where men could see them. Ma-aui, who fished up the Great Island of Hawaii, snared the Sun and made him go more slowly across the heavens so more heat could get to plants and fruits. Ma-aui, who won fire for men from Ma-hui'a's fingernail and overcame Kuna Loa the Long Eel who tried to kill his mother and almost won immortality for men from the great goblin goddess, Hina-of-the-Night, by taking the heart out of her body, diving down her throat past teeth as sharp as fiery glass of volcano, after giving warning to birds not to sing until I came out. Ma-aui, who went down into the goblin's stomach, seized her heart and got as far as her jaws when a bird—Paka-kai, the water wagtail—became excited and sang. The Goblin Goddess woke up, and the Meat of Immortality slipped through my hands and back into her.

MARTY: Cowabunga, dude! You are one action-Jackson! So tell us more about this "thing" between you and the Goblin Goddess.

MA-AUI: *(bows, sits)* I exist solely for *ka maika'i o ka 'aina*—the goodness of the land. Hawaii is *k-u'u ipo*—my sweetheart. *Ua aloha au iaia*— I love her and have died many times to protect her from evildoers.

(He brandishes his knife and starts toward MARTY; SANDY steps between them and pulls MARTY away with her to center stage; MA-AUI returns to seat.)

SANDY: Speaking of tropical destinations, Marty, this is the time of year a lot of viewers are thinking of taking a vacation cruise. Old Stormalong is one of the world's truly legendary sea captains…two hundred-twenty years old and still at the helm of his giant clipper ship, *The Courser*. I heard you say backstage you were in Europe recently?

OLD STORMALONG: Aaargh, lassie, right you are. We were in the North Atlantic headed from Nantucket to Liverpool, when we hit the granddaddy of all storms. There were clouds and fog, and the sky got as black as balled pitch. Not a thing could be seen; why, the sun didn't come out for two weeks. When it did, I found the ship had been blown up by the gulfstream and carried clear over England into the North Sea hard by Norway. The only way to get back to the Atlantic was through the English Channel, but *The Courser* was too broad in the beam. I climbed up the rigging of the main mast and looked ahead. On one side was France, the other England, with the steep, craggy Cliffs of Dover looming high overhead. I eyeballed the channel width and could see the ship was an inch narrower. "It'll be a tight squeeze," says I, so I ordered the crew to soap the sides so she could squeeze through easy-like, a mite more on the starboard side, soaped up and down till the ship was slick as glass. Well, we cast off, and when we hit the Channel, she squeaked and scraped, and all the soap on the starboard rubbed off on the Dover side, but we made it with nary an inch to spare. And that's why the Cliffs of Dover are white to this very day!

MARTY: Gosh, and *I* thought it was vandals. Yuk-yuk-yuk! Well, let's look in on the wonderful world of wildlife with our resident tall tale Texan, Big-Foot Wallace, Captain of the Original Texas Rangers!

BIG-FOOT WALLACE: By the great horn spoon, I want to tell you about spiders. Now, all the spiders in Texas are as big as a brick, and their bite is invariably fatal. The only cure is to listen to music. At the end of a day's work chasing horse thieves and outlaws, we Rangers would be all stove up with spider bites, so we'd ride full-teakettle to the station house where a big brass band would be playing. Now, the Santafy spider was the deadliest. It had a hundred legs and a sting in every leg and a forked tail with a sting in each fork and a mouth that had fangs bigger than a rattlesnake. If it stung a man he might live an hour; if it hit him with all its legs he'd be dead in fifteen minutes, turning blue, then yellow, then green, then dead. One day I was out in the West Texas plains where the winds blow so stiff a man has to lean over till he is nearly horizontal just to stand. I'd been lassoing cyclones with Pecos Bill. You shoulda seen old Bill fan those cyclones with his hat, then kick a streak of lighting out of the way and hop on! Oh, those cyclones would rear and buck, trying to throw him. They couldn't, of course, so they'd rained out from under him, and one time in California, Pecos Bill hit the ground so hard, he drove the ground a hundred feet below sea level. He called it Death Valley, and it's still there. Well, sure enough, as I was headed home, I got bit by a Santafy spider and got set to die in five minutes or so. Then I heard a sound like a clarinet. I saw where the wind had blown a knothole right through one of those post oaks, and the air was rushing through the hole so that it made a musical note. There was another pop, then another, till a whole bunch of pops and notes sounded and arranged themselves into a tune. And what do you think that tune was, sonny?

MARTY: Uhhhh, *Bite Me Daddy Eight to the Bar?* Yuk-yuk-yuk!

BIG-FOOT WALLACE: The tune was *The Yellow Rose of Texas.* Finally, I heard enough of the tune to be cured, and I sang it all the way back to Austin. *(sings)* There's a yellow rose in Texas that I am going to see; no other Ranger knows her, no other, only me—

(ANNOUNCER holds up "Cut to Commercial" sign.)

MARTY: Thanks, Big-Foot. We'll be back with more *America Blabs!* after this absurd and relatively unimportant message from our sponsor.

(ANNOUNCER holds up "Applause" sign; AUDIENCE applauds, GUESTS murmur among themselves. SANDY pulls MARTY to her and confers privately.)

SANDY: I'm getting the word from management. They want more "intellectual interchange."

MARTY: More screaming?

SANDY: More fighting.

MARTY: More senseless name-calling and adolescent hair-pulling?

SANDY: More chair-throwing and shin-kicking.

MARTY: Well, that should be easy to arrange. Here on *America Blabs!*, tantrums 'r' us!

(ANNOUNCER holds up "Applause" sign; AUDIENCE applauds.)

ANNOUNCER: And we're back! With the nation's favorite co-dependent co-hosts, Sandy Starr and Marty Million!

(Applause fades.)

SANDY: Representing the blue-collar working person's perspective, we have John Henry and Joe Magarac. Joe, you're a recent immigrant to the United States. In fact, you were specifically created by U. S. Steel Corporation in 1930 for use in an advertising campaign.

JOE MAGARAC: *(rolls up sleeves, flexes muscles)* You betcha, Sandy! I come from Slovakia to McKeesport, Pennsylvan-i-a. Everybody laugh and say: "Magarac! That is some name! In Slovak it means "jackass." You are Joe Jackass Donkey! Ha-ha-ha!" How they laugh. I laugh and say, "You betcha," I say. "I am *magarac* for sure and work like jackass donkey. I am real steel man…*(opens up shirt)* made of solid steel.

AUDIENCE: Wow! Ooh! Incredible!

JOE MAGARAC: I show you how Joe Magarac works. *(mimes motions)* I pick up handful of steel, squeeze out eight rails at a time between my fingers, each A-Number One perfect. I throw whole train cars of limestone, scrap iron and ore into furnace, stick hands in furnace, stir hot steel around, take a little taste…mmm-mmm good…and pretty soon this steel be cooked up good, you betcha! *(laughs heartily)*

SANDY: Of course, Mr. Magarac, you've had some criticism for functioning simply as a propaganda tool for the corporate exploitation of workers.

(ANNOUNCER holds up "Boo-Hiss" sign; AUDIENCE boos, hisses.)

JOE MAGARAC: *(frowns, stands)* I tell you story, Sandy. One time the bosses were going to shut down mill…put workers out of work for long time, no paydays, no money for food or clothes, babies get sick and die, hard times for working people. Bosses say they could not find right kind of steel—maybe true, maybe not. No matter to Joe Magarac. I hop into ladle, start up furnace, melt myself down to make best steel for new mill. And when steel is made, they pour out steel with me in it, roll it into beams and girders and make biggest new mill you ever saw, you betcha! Joe Magarac—one good man for making steel and saving workers' jobs!

(He sits, shakes hands with OLD STORMALONG and JOHN HENRY as BIG-FOOT WALLACE and MA-AUI nod assent and WHITE PAINTED WOMAN beats her drum to AUDIENCE applause.)

SANDY: Now, Mr. Henry, like Big-Foot Wallace, you were a genuinely real person that became a folk legend.

JOHN HENRY: Yes, ma'am, I surely was. That's because I was a natural man. I could drill more holes and drill 'em deeper than any other man on the railroad. I drill the holes, the dynamite go in—blammity-wham-blam! Tunnel come through. That's because I was a natural man. I had a hammer in each hand and a mouthful of spikes. I'd spit out the spikes—thew! thew!—and swing those hammers down—whop! whop!—and pound down those ties just ahead of a steaming train. In 1871 when the C&O Railroad was building through West Virginia, this salesman come up to the track boss and try to sell him a steam drill. Boss said, "I got a man here, a natural man named John Henry, can beat that steam drill every time." Salesman and the boss place a bet. Salesman said, "No man can beat a machine!" I said, "He can if he's a natural man!" *(stands, mimes motions with hammers)* Well, the drill start up, and the drill keep on turning. My sweet Polly Ann, she said, "John Henry, that hammer gonna be the death of you!" But John Henry, he keep on driving—whop!—keep on driving into that rock-hard mountain—whop!—sun went high in the sky—whop!—sun went low in the sky—whop!—steam drill keep on turning, John Henry keep on driving—whop!—before he'd let that steam drill beat him down, he'd die with his hammer in his hand—whop!—till all of a sudden John Henry break through the rock, and he have twice as many holes drilled cleaner and deeper than that steam drill! Yes, ma'am, I beat that machine—beat it because I was a natural man!

(JOHN HENRY bows, sits; AUDIENCE applauds.)

SANDY: That's a very exciting tale, Mr. Henry, but some revisionist historians have suggested that you were, in fact, a strike breaker—

MARTY: "Scab" is the word most commonly used, I believe.

SANDY: —whose manic need for reckless self-promotion actually endangered the safety of your co-workers. How would you respond to those allegations?

(ANNOUNCER holds up "Boo-Hiss" sign; AUDIENCE boos, hisses.)

JOHN HENRY: *(laughs)* Ma'am, a natural man doesn't have to do a thing but be himself. I don't guess you modern folks can understand, but we legends, we "tall tales," as you call us, didn't come about to satisfy some fancy theories or sell books or just entertain folks like you do here. All the things we did in our legends were what regular people wanted to do in their own lives—but couldn't. Cause they were poor. Or weak. Or scared. We rose up because the people needed someone like us to be there…for them. To stand up when they were beat down. To fight when they were defenseless. To make sense out of world that a lot of times made no sense at all.

SANDY: *(to audience)* Well, you heard it straight from the horse's mouth. Audience, it's time for your thoughts.

MARTY: Over here, Sandy!

(He holds a microphone up to AUDIENCE MEMBER #1, who stands.)

AUDIENCE MEMBER #1: I have a question for White Painted Woman and Ma-aui. Like, you two are thousands, maybe millions of years old. How do you keep in shape? Do you have, like, really excellent personal trainers? *(sits)*

WHITE PAINTED WOMAN: We stay strong because of the belief you have in us. When your belief in legend weakens, the world becomes ever more shallow in its soul, ever more empty in its heart.

AUDIENCE MEMBER #2: *(stands, grabs microphone)* Hold on! You expect us to believe you're responsible for introducing thunder and lightning and rain into the world? And that the reason the human race has fire is because this wacko surfer guy stole it from some other wacko guy's fingernail? Hey, have I got some great oceanfront property in the Grand Canyon for you! *(sits)*

WHITE PAINTED WOMAN: I created that canyon. You have no right to sell it.

(AUDIENCE applauds.)

MA-AUI: *(stands)* *Hoaloha.* Friend, how do *you* think the human race obtained fire?

AUDIENCE MEMBER #2: Well, according to scientists—

MA-AUI: Ah, scientists! They speak of microbes and molecules. Tiny, invisible creatures that control the world—your world and everything in it. *I* speak of great monsters who devour whole villages in a single bite. In both cases, you are in peril. Do you rest more easily because your enemy is small and unseen? Are you in less danger because you believe your mortal illness is caused by bacteria instead of giant goblins? *(sits)*

BIG-FOOT WALLACE: I think what the gentleman from Hawaii is trying to say is, you've created us tall tales precisely because science *doesn't* give you all the answers. Even after it tells you in meticulous detail *how* the world works, it won't answer the really big question of *why*. And human beings just can't go on living unless we have some sort of piebald, jerry-rigged explanation of why we're here in the first place.

SANDY: We'd like to remind you viewers at home that you can call in to *America Blabs!*, where you're live with Big-Foot Wallace!

AUDIENCE MEMBER #3: *(stands)* I'd like to ask Big-Foot if he's related to that other Big-Foot dude, the one that's like a yeti and all hairy and eats sheep and stuff? *(sits)*

BIG-FOOT WALLACE: *(chuckles)* No, 'fraid not, pardner. But that's an interesting legend, isn't it? You know why it still persists, even though nobody's ever actually seen the creature? Because if our world gets too tame and too explained, folks won't have anything to do with their minds. The day the human race stops making up Big-Foots and yetis and Loch Ness Monsters is the day we might as well just not bother waking up.

AUDIENCE MEMBER #4: *(stands)* Then you're all just figments of our imagination? *(sits)*

JOE MAGARAC: *(stands, fists clenched)* I am no figment! I am every American man and woman who has sweated and bled in steel mill!

OLD STORMALONG: *(stands)* I'm every sailor that ever gave his life to the raging sea!

JOHN HENRY: *(stands)* And I'm every American who helped build this country and whose contribution to the wealth and freedom we enjoy today was never recognized. There were millions of those folks, and you may have forgotten them, every one.

BIG-FOOT WALLACE: *(stands)* But you won't forget *us*. Cause we're tall tales, and every time you tell our story—

WHITE PAINTED: *(stands)* You celebrate your ancestors...

MA-AUI: *(stands)* And the heroes of today. What legends will celebrate them?

JOE MAGARAC: Who will Americans of tomorrow turn to in time of need?

OLD STORMALONG: Barbie and Ken?

JOHN HENRY: Homer Simpson?

BIG-FOOT WALLACE: Grievous and Mutthead?

MARTY: Gosh-a-rooni, sports fans, it sure won't be us, will it, Sandy?

SANDY: No way, Jose! We only have a combined attention span of fifteen seconds!

MARTY: Isn't that amazing?

SANDY: What is?

MARTY: I don't know. I've already forgotten!

(SANDY and MARTY laugh hysterically. ANNOUNCER holds up "30 Sec." sign. SANDY and MARTY step to down center and face front. THE TALL TALES descend from dais and gather behind SANDY and MARTY.)

MARTY: Thank you for joining this edition of *America Blabs!*

SANDY: For "America's Tall Tales: Where Are They Now?"

(JOE MAGARAC pokes MARTY in the shoulder; JOHN HENRY pokes MARTY in the other shoulder.)

MARTY: Uhhh, they're right behind us, Sandy.

SANDY: Thanks a million, Marty!

MARTY: No, I mean they really are right behind us. Hey, what gives?

(ANNOUNCER holds up "Applause" sign; AUDIENCE applauds. SOUND: CANNED AUDIENCE APPLAUSE. BIG-FOOT WALLACE pulls his six-gun and directs JOE MAGARAC and JOHN HENRY as they pick up MARTY and hustle him offstage left. WHITE PAINTED WOMAN stuffs kerchief in SANDY'S mouth, MA-AUI ties her hands behind her back. OLD STORMALONG shakes hands with AUDIENCE. LIGHTS OUT.)

THE END

GRETA NILSON'S
MAGIC MARE
(La Caballa Blanca)

La Caballa Blanca is based upon a Blackfoot tribal legend about Shunka-tonka-Wakan—"the Ghost Horse." The Ghost Horse is known in Western frontier folkore under many names: Pacing White Mustang, Phantom Wild Horse, White Steed of the Prairies, White Sultan. Tales about a mysterious, uncatchable white mustang appearing at inexplicable moments to assist or confound humans have been in oral circulation throughout the West since the time of the Spanish Conquistadors; an early written mention from 1832 occurs in Washington Irving's *A Tour on the Prairies*. This version highlights the frequent folklore motif of how nature's powerful forces may be harnessed only by persons pure of heart—an idea that also forms the heart of another of the world's most ancient and enduring quests, the search for The Holy Grail.

TIME: August, 1852

PLACE: On the Oregon Trail, midway between the North Platte and the Little Medicine Bow Rivers

CAST: Greta Nilson   Mary Lennox
         Zeke Lennox   Olaf Nilson, Greta's father
         Yellow Hawk   Jim Bridger
         3 Conquistadors   Captain Brannan
         Ingrid Nilson, Greta's mother

STAGE SET: Conestoga wagon; boulders; bedroll

PROPS: journal book; quill pen; three Conquistador swords; kindling; two Spanish coins

SPECIAL EFFECTS: sound—horse hooves, wind whistling, thunder, Indian drums, bird whistle, lightning; visual—lightning

MUSIC: *Buscando la Quinta Pata al Gato; La Polverita Fiera*

COSTUMES: characters dress in mid-19th-century frontier clothes; Yellow Hawk wears moccasins, fringed shirt and breeches; soldiers dress in conquistador outfits with swords, helmets, armor

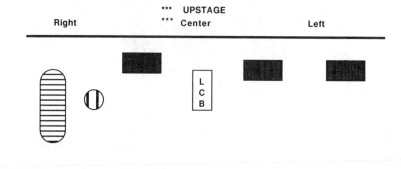

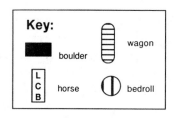

Stage Plan -- *La Caballa Blanca*
(Greta Nilson's Magic Mare)

(MUSIC: "Buscando la Quinta Pata al Gato" played slowly by violin. LIGHTS UP STAGE RIGHT on a group of people arranged in front of a Conestoga wagon. CAPTAIN BRANNAN and JIM BRIDGER, leaders of the wagon train, stand together at extreme down right, coffee cups in hand; ZEKE LENNOX tosses restlessly on his bedroll a few feet to the left of BRANNAN and BRIDGER, attended by his wife, MARY LENNOX, who is writing in her journal; behind THE LENNOXES stand OLAF and INGRID NILSON, husband and wife, hanging their heads in sadness. MUSIC FADES OUT.)

MARY LENNOX: *(writing in journal)* Diary of Mary Lennox, September the fourteenth, year of our Lord 18 and 52. This wagon train of two hundred-fifty hardy immigrants bound for the Oregon Territory may have reached trail's end sooner than expected. In an effort to cross the mountains before the onset of winter, we have strayed from the main trail and find ourselves amid the arid foothills of eastern Wyoming. Our supplies are nearly depleted and our leaders, Captain Brannan and the famous mountain man Jim Bridger, struggle to maintain discipline among the frightened teamsters. We have seen no sign of fresh water nor the smallest hint of rain for over a hundred miles. And each day another of us falls victim to a mysterious pestilence that sweeps through the camp like a bitter, killing wind. My husband, Zeke, is so enfeebled he can scarce raise a trembling hand to his fevered brow. Even the fierce Blackfoot and Cheyenne—in whose lands we unavoidably trespass—keep a wary distance, as if we had already crossed into the world of the dead.

(SOUND: Indian drum, up for several seconds, then fade under dialogue.)

MARY LENNOX: And, as the leaders of the company meet to decide our next course of action, yet more tragic news is received.

(An anxious INGRID NILSON clutches the hand of OLAF NILSON, who leads her around THE LENNOXES to CAPTAIN BRANNAN and JIM BRIDGER.)

INGRID NILSON: Olaf! What are we going to do?

OLAF NILSON: Ingrid, you must be calm. We will find her.

CAPTAIN BRANNAN: Nilson, ma'am. What's the matter?

OLAF NILSON: It is our daughter, Captain. Greta is gone from the train.

CAPTAIN BRANNAN: Gone?

INGRID NILSON: She has been stolen by savages! *(sobs)*

OLAF NILSON: Please. I beg your pardon, gentlemen. My wife is talking wild. But our Greta, she is only fourteen. We have looked everywhere.

JIM BRIDGER: That's all right, folks. We'll find your daughter. I've trapped and scouted in this country since Lewis and Clark, and I ain't never lost a traveler yet. When did you see the girl last?

OLAF NILSON: Just before we go to sleep, Greta say she is too awake! She say the sound of a flute is in her ears.

INGRID NILSON: And something about a horse!

(MUSIC: first two bars of "La Polverita Fiera" played by flute, pause, then repeated as if a summons. SPOTLIGHT UP CENTER ON

GRETA NILSON, entering from behind wagon as if sleepwalking; entranced by the music, she wanders left, following the sound.)

OLAF NILSON: But we see no horse.

INGRID NILSON: And this morning, Greta is gone!

CAPTAIN BRANNAN: You folks go back to your wagon. I'll send Bridger out with a search party.

OLAF NILSON: Thank you, Captain, Mr. Bridger. *(NILSONS exit right)*

JIM BRIDGER: Captain, the only chance for any of us to make it through before the snow is to keep moving. The longer we delay, the weaker we get.

CAPTAIN BRANNAN: I know, Bridger. But did you see the anguish on their faces? Their four-year-old son died last year on the voyage over from Sweden. And now their daughter…

JIM BRIDGER: I'll have a looksee, Captain, but I don't reckon we'll find her.

CAPTAIN BRANNAN: Indians?

JIM BRIDGER: Naw! I've lived among these tribes for nigh thirty years, and they ain't after our scalps. In fact, her best chance for survival is if the Indians *do* find her. No, Captain, it's the fever that done it. It's made these poor folks crazy in the head. Greta Nilson just wandered off…could be twenty miles away by now at the bottom of a ravine…or breakfast for a pack of coyotes. We'll never find her alive. *(hangs head, exits right with BRANNAN)*

(LIGHTS OUT; MARY and ZEKE LENNOX go behind wagon. LIGHTS UP CENTER AND LEFT ON GRETA moving slowly around stage, searching. SOUND: horse hooves in near distance. GRETA hears hooves and takes shelter behind the boulder at up left, peering above it as if expecting a horse to pass by; the sound fades, and she emerges and crosses to center stage. A bird whistle sounds from behind her, and she turns.)

GRETA: Oh, please…please come out! Do not be afraid! I will not harm you!

(A Blackfoot Indian boy, YELLOW HAWK, comes out from behind boulder at up right.)

GRETA NILSON: My name is Greta. I am from Sweden.

YELLOW HAWK: I am called Yellow Hawk. My father is chief of Blackfoot.

(They circle each other, matching each other's motions and gestures—raising hands, turning right and left, rising up and down—then stop when they hear music and look left toward sound. MUSIC: first two bars of "La Polverita Fiera" played by flute, pause, then repeated.)

GRETA NILSON: That lovely music! I have been following it since last night!

YELLOW HAWK: It is the voice of Shunka-tonka-Wakan—"the Ghost Horse."

GRETA NILSON: Ghost horse?

YELLOW HAWK: The most noble white mustang with silver mane and tail. When Ghost Horse appears, she makes no sound, but there is music in the air, music of the heavens from where she comes. She can be seen at night only, her mane and tail shining bright like the moon, her head and body flying through the air like a white fiery arrow burning the sky.

GFRETA NILSON: Where does she live?

YELLOW HAWK: Everywhere the wind blows. She travels by night from Canada to Mexico. Long time ago, men searching for gold brought her from Spain and called her "La Caballa Blanca." They believed she would lead them to El Dorado and the Seven Cities of Gold. But their hearts were deep with evil. They never found their treasure, and the mare ran away. Blackfoot legend say Ghost Horse will never be ridden except by one of pure heart.

GRETA NILSON: I would like to ride her!

YELLOW HAWK: Ride her? *(guffaws)* Few have even seen her. No one has ever caught her. Not brave or squaw. Not white man or Indian.

GRETA NILSON: She is calling me. I have been hearing her for days along the trail. Have you ever seen her, Yellow Hawk?

YELLOW HAWK: Two moons ago, my father took me to hunt wild horses. Like wolves, wild horses very curious animals. They will follow men for miles, always traveling ahead but then turning back to watch us. They have the kind of courage a man has—to face anything he can see. One night we followed a herd into a canyon. Slowly we crept toward them. Suddenly, Ghost Horse stood on the mesa above, her music singing to the herd below, telling them to escape.

(MUSIC: last two bars of "La Polverita Fiera," section A, played by flute.)

GRETA NILSON: There it is! Oh, caballa blanca, where are you?

YELLOW HAWK: Come. I will take you back to your people now. You have wandered far.

GRETA NILSON: No, I must find her!

(MUSIC: "Buscando la Quinta Pata al Gato" played slowly by violin. THREE MEN in 16th-century Spanish conquistador uniforms enter from left and cross to GRETA and YELLOW HAWK at center.)

SOLDIER #1: Buenas tardes, señor y señorita. *(bows)* I am Francisco Coronado, humble servant of King Phillip of Spain. Have you perchance seen una caballa blanca? A beautiful white horse? We have been seeking this beast for a very long time.

YELLOW HAWK: We have not seen her, Capítan.

SOLDIER #1: *(brandishes his sword)* Well, we *shall* find her. Find her and break her, for the glory of His Majesty the King! Oh, this animal is wily, amigos. I believe she is the devil's own foal. She has eluded me and many others into eternity, but we shall soon find her *and* the treasure she so cleverly conceals in El Dorado.

GRETA NILSON: *(steps forward)* Begging your pardon, Señor Coronado, but you will never find La Caballa Blanca—nor your ill-favored riches. Not in *this* land, anyway. *This* is a land of freedom. A land of honesty and goodness. A land built on a new foundation of faith and hope, where God does not favor the rich or high-born but the hard-working, humble tiller of the field and the skilled, dutiful crafter of handwork. You seek only to despoil and ravage this land, to make it submit to conquest. La Caballa Blanca will never show you her treasure. Never!

(THE THREE SOLDIERS grasp their weapons.)

SOLDIER #1: Heresy! Mi bonita, you must have a talk with our esteemed Grand Inquisitor—

(MUSIC: the first two bars of "Buscando la Quinta Pata al Gato" played slowly by violin. SOLDIERS harken to the sound and look right.)

SOLDIER #2: I heard it! The horse! It came from over there! *(points right)*

SOLDIER #3: No, it was that way! *(points left)*

SOLDIER #1: Follow me! *(charges offstage left, followed by other SOLDIERS)*

GRETA NILSON: I heard only the wind.

YELLOW HAWK: It is nightfall. I will find shelter. *(goes behind up right boulder)*

(LIGHTS DIM. SOUND: WIND WHISTLING, THEN MUSIC: "La Polverita Fiera" played by flute. SOUND: THUNDER. LIGHTS OUT BRIEFLY, STROBE, THEN UP FULL CENTER as the center boulder cover has been removed to reveal La Caballa Blanca.)

GRETA NILSON: The mare! La Caballa Blanca!

(She waltzes around it as if it were her dance partner; as music ends, she mounts the horse. YELLOW HAWK returns with kindling.)

YELLOW HAWK: Shunka-tonka-Wakan! The magic mare has come!

(He walks around GRETA and the horse in awe, then kneels. LIGHTS STROBE.)

YELLOW HAWK: You are a great spirit! Pure of heart!

GRETA NILSON: She wants to run, Yellow Hawk! What must I do?

YELLOW HAWK: Follow her where she takes you.

GRETA NILSON: Where will she go?

YELLOW HAWK: Where you want to be. The Ghost Horse already knows.

GRETA NILSON: Away then! Fast away!

(YELLOW HAWK trots offstage left. LIGHTS OUT, THEN SPOT-LIGHT ON GRETA RIDING HORSE. SOUND: THUNDER, LIGHTNING. MUSIC: "La Polverita Fiera," B Section, played by flute. LIGHTS OUT, GRETA slips off horse and behind it; horse is covered with boulder cloth. LIGHTS UP RIGHT on the Conestoga wagon. CAPTAIN BRANNAN and JIM BRIDGER stand together at extreme down right with a grieving OLAF and INGRID NILSON; a smiling, stretching ZEKE LENNOX sits up on his bedroll a few feet to the left, next to his wife, MARY LENNOX, who is writing in her journal. MUSIC FADES OUT.)

MARY LENNOX: *(writing in journal)* September the fifteenth. Some good news. My husband Zeke has recovered to where he can drive our wagon. And a brief cloudburst passed over us last night, lending a few drops to our dessicated canteens. But the young Swedish girl has not been found, and it is time to move on.

CAPTAIN BRANNAN: *(to NILSONS)* I'm sorry, folks. If Jim Bridger couldn't find your daughter, well then, she can't be found. For your sake, and for the rest of us, we've got to saddle up.

INGRID NILSON: *(sobs)* My poor Greta!

(GRETA appears standing at center stage.)

GRETA NILSON: Mama! Papa! Why is everyone so sad?
INGRID NILSON: Oh, Greta!

(INGRID and OLAF rush to GRETA and hug her.)

JIM BRIDGER: You're mighty lucky, little lady. We were just about to hit the trail.

CAPTAIN BRANNAN: All right, people, we don't have time to gawk! Get ready to move out and head south!

GRETA NILSON: Wait! Don't go that way. In thirty miles you'll end up in a box canyon, and you'll be trapped. We have to go north. *(points to left)* Just over that ridge we'll come to a river and an easy ford, then there's a pass through the mountains. Plenty of water along the way. We can make it across just before the snows come.

JIM BRIDGER: Beggin' my pardon, young miss, but you must have taken a mighty hard fall on your noggin out there. These maps don't show anything north of here but desert and rocks.

GRETA NILSON: But I saw it! I saw the trail! La Caballa Blanca showed it to me.

CAPTAIN BRANNAN: La Caballa Blanca? The White Mustang? *(chuckles)* That's just an old Indian tale.

GRETA NILSON: But I rode her! We rode for hundreds of miles. I saw so many wonderful sights.

OLAF NILSON: Greta, you are talking nonsense!

GRETA NILSON: Then what about these? I found them last night.

(She opens her hand to reveal two coins, shows them to BRANNAN and BRIDGER.)

CAPTAIN BRANNAN: Lennox, you've been to school. You recognize this wampum?

ZEKE LENNOX: *(examines coins)* These are Spanish coins, Captain. Look like 17th, maybe 16th century. How in the world they'd show up around here, I have no idea.

JIM BRIDGER: You know, Captain, I might be wrong about that southern route. If the trail really is just over that ridge, like the girl says, well, we wouldn't lose that much time havin' a looksee.

GRETA NILSON: It *is* there! I know it is!

CAPTAIN BRANNAN: *(looks from GRETA to BRIDGER and back again)* Bridger, take two men and scout ahead. Lennox, Nilson, let's get these wagons turned around. We're heading due north—next stop Oregon!

BRIDGER, OLAF & INGRID NILSON, ZEKE LENNOX: Hurrah! Oregon or bust!

(BRIDGER and BRANNAN exit right, followed by ZEKE and MARY LENNOX, then OLAF and INGRID and GRETA, who casts a last look toward the horse/boulder at center stage. LIGHTS OUT, THEN SPOTLIGHT CENTER ON LA CABALLA BLANCA. MUSIC: "La Polverita Fiera" played by flute and violin under dialogue.)

MARY LENNOX: *(o.s.) (writing in journal)* October the nineteenth, 18 and 52. We have at last reached the verdant, promised land of Oregon, losing not a single immigrant since crossing through the mountain pass five weeks ago. As we kneel to thank Providence for our salvation, there are many among us who credit another source of deliverance—the faith of young Greta Nilson and the divine mercy of her proud, magic mare.

(MUSIC up then out. SPOTLIGHT OUT.)

THE END

La Polverita Fiera
(by L.E. McCullough)

© L.E. McCullough 1996

Buscando la Quinta Pata al Gato
(by L.E. McCullough)

© L.E. McCullough 1996

WHEN PEOPLE COULD FLY

When People Could Fly is based upon an African-American folktale created sometime before the Civil War. While it gives a prominent role to the practice of magic, it is really a story about ordinary men and women having the strength to endure the unendurable and gain respite from the world's cruelty by harnessing the spiritual knowledge that lies within us. Though this is a play based on the all too real institution of American slavery, there is no need for all actors to be "ethnically correct." In fact, using a bit of non-traditional casting, with Caucasian or non-African-American students playing the parts of slaves and non-Caucasians appearing as slavers, may make for an even more moving drama.

TIME: Slavery Time in America: 1619-1865

PLACE: a plantation in the Deep South

CAST: Sleepy John   Overseer
          Cato   Master
          Rachel   8 Africans

STAGE SET: painted backgrounds of cotton fields, trees, blue skies, mansion, Africa; row of cotton sacks

PROPS: Rachel's baby; Overseer's whip; Master's pistol; 10 cotton sacks; guitar

SPECIAL EFFECTS: sound—trumpet call; pistol shots

MUSIC: African drumming; songs—*Where Will I Be When the First Trumpet Sounds?; Go Down, Hannah; Hey, Rattler, Hey*

COSTUMES: characters dress in mid-19th-century clothes with appropriate class and occupational distinctions: slaves are in ragged field dress, Overseer and Master wear nicely-cut trousers, shirts and jackets; Africans in Africa wear colorful robes and cloaks; Sleepy John can dress as a modern blues singer

Stage Plan -- *When People Could Fly*

Key:

⬭ cotton sack   ▬ scrim

(LIGHTS UP. At stage right is a man sitting on a chair; he plays the melody to "Where Shall I Be When the First Trumpet Sounds?" on a guitar, slowly and with a bottleneck or slide if possible. He stops and looks at the audience.)

SLEEPY JOHN: They call me Sleepy John. Sleepy John the Tell Man, cause I got all kinds of tells in my guitar here. Some of my tells is from time long, long ago. Did you know, there was a time when people could fly? Long ago in Africa, some people knew a special kind of magic. With this magic, they would sprout wings and walk up in the air and in the clouds just like climbing a fence, and they would fly like birds over the trees and plains.

(EIGHT AFRICANS wearing colorful robes and cloaks dance onstage from left, whirling all across the stage in a lilting, romping dance of joy and carefree abandon that lasts from 30-45 seconds. MUSIC: African drumming, continuing until end of dance.)

SLEEPY JOHN: Then an evil time came—many of the African people were captured for slavery.

(AFRICANS fall down, throw off their robes and cloaks and crawl to center stage where they are herded together by the OVERSEER; they kneel in a straight line across the stage, heads bowed, OVERSEER pacing in front of them. Marking the row are cotton sacks they sling over their shoulders.)

SLEEPY JOHN: And when they got loaded up on the slave ships to be taken across the ocean to the Western lands, they got sick and forgot about their magic. Pretty soon in the land of America, the heat of the sun and the sting of the whip made them forget they ever knew any magic at all.

(AFRICANS begin working ground with hands, as if digging a crop row. MUSIC: "Go Down, Hannah" sung by AFRICANS.)

AFRICANS: *(sing)*
Why don't you go down old Hannah
Well, well, well
Don't you rise no more
Don't you rise no more
Why don't you go down old Hannah
Don't you rise no more

(OVERSEER beckons offstage left, and CATO and RACHEL enter, RACHEL carrying a bundled baby; OVERSEER directs them to line up with other slaves and assume digging posture. OVERSEER walks to up left, turns back on slaves; CATO stands and spreads his arms out in front of him.)

SLEEPY JOHN: But some of the people kept their magic, though they no longer walked around with wings. They looked the same as the other African folks who had been made slaves, but they were different. There was one old man called Cato. He was wise, and the other slaves respected him. Looked upon him as their teacher, even though they were forbidden to learn to read or be educated. Forbidden to do anything but what the man who called himself Master wanted them to do.

(MASTER enters from left, sees RACHEL, beckons to OVERSEER and points to RACHEL; OVERSEER nudges RACHEL with his whip to get up and go to MASTER. MASTER touches her arm, then shoulder and RACHEL pulls away. MASTER beckons OVERSEER, who grabs baby from a protesting RACHEL and gives it to MASTER, who exits left. OVERSEER directs RACHEL back to her place and walks back to his spot up left. With CATO starting up song and singing lead, AFRICANS sing "Hey, Rattler!" using body percussion and striking rhythm on the floor with their hands.)

(verse)
CATO: *(sings)* When I first come over across the sea
AFRICANS: *(sing)* Hey, rattler, hey
CATO: *(sings)* Come to the land of liberty
AFRICANS: *(sing)* Hey, rattler, hey
CATO: *(sings)* All I see is folks in chains
AFRICANS: *(sing)* Hey, rattler, hey
CATO: *(sings)* Spend their life in fear and pain
AFRICANS: *(sing)* Hey, rattler, hey

(chorus)
CATO: *(sings)* Well, it's hey, hey, rattler
AFRICANS: *(sing)* Hey, rattler, hey
CATO: *(sings)* Well, it's hey, hey, rattler
AFRICANS: *(sing)* Hey, rattler, hey

(verse)
CATO: *(sings)* I got trouble, trouble in mind
AFRICANS: *(sing)* Hey, rattler, hey
CATO: *(sings)* If trouble don't kill me, I'll live a long time
AFRICANS: *(sing)* Hey, rattler, hey
CATO: *(sings)* Spread my wings, gonna fly away home
AFRICANS: *(sing)* Hey, rattler, hey
CATO: *(sings)* When I reach that cloud, I'll be long gone
AFRICANS: *(sing)* Hey, rattler, hey

(chorus)
CATO: *(sings)* Well, it's hey, hey, rattler
AFRICANS: *(sing)* Hey, rattler, hey

CATO: *(sings)* Well, it's hey, hey, rattler
AFRICANS: *(sing)* Hey, rattler, hey

> *(Singing ends; during last chorus RACHEL has weakened and collapses. A few AFRICANS get up to assist but OVERSEER waves them back down again with his whip. He gestures for CATO to bring RACHEL out to where he stands at left of row. When RACHEL is in front of him, he whips her, then motions for CATO to take her back in the row. OVERSEER begins clapping in rhythmic time, and AFRICANS begin digging motions to the rhythm. OVERSEER speeds up rhythm, AFRICANS speed up digging. RACHEL falls out again and collapses. OVERSEER motions for CATO to bring her to him and readies his whip.)*

CATO: *(stands and addresses the prone RACHEL)* Child of Africa, the time has come. You must raise your wings and fly…heed the trumpet's call and fly to the land of our ancestors. Fly to the land called Freedom!

> *(SOUND: trumpet call offstage.)*

RACHEL: The words, brother! Tell the magic sky words!
CATO: The power is within you, sister. Kana kali…maneka macombe… sihana saluke! Power…within you.
RACHEL: *(haltingly)* Kana kali…maneka macombe…sihana saluke!
CATO & RACHEL: Kana kali…maneka macombe…sihana saluke! Kana kali…maneka macombe…sihana saluke!

> *(RACHEL rises, pulls a brightly-colored scarf from her cotton sack, puts it around her head and neck and dances offstage left past the startled OVERSEER. She begins her dance slowly, clumsily, then glides rapidly and with great joy and ease. MUSIC: African drumming continuing to RACHEL'S exit. SOUND: trumpet call offstage. OVERSEER brandishes whip and paces in front of AFRICANS.)*

OVERSEER: Now…you people…neither you nor I…saw *anything* unusual. No…one…saw…*anything!* Y'all hear me? And of all the things you did *not* see, you most of all did *not* see a woman sprout wings and fly across the fields over yonder!

> *(OVERSEER retreats back to his position up left as AFRICANS resume digging motions.)*

SLEEPY JOHN: Next day killing hot. And the next the same and same and same again. The man who called himself Master wanted more work from his slaves, more blood from their bodies, more money from their blood. *(MUSIC: "Go Down, Hannah" sung by AFRICANS.)*

AFRICANS: *(sing)*

Why don't you go down old Hannah
Well, well, well
Don't you rise no more
Don't you rise no more
Why don't you go down old Hannah
Don't you rise no more

(Music stops. An AFRICAN weakens and collapses; OVERSEER has CATO drag the AFRICAN to him and raises his whip. CATO recites the magic sky words.)

CATO: Kana kali…maneka macombe…sihana saluke! Kana kali… maneka macombe…sihana saluke!

AFRICAN: *(slowly, weakly)* Kana kali…maneka macombe…sihana saluke!

CATO & AFRICAN: Kana kali…maneka macombe…sihana saluke! Kana kali…maneka macombe…sihana saluke!

(AFRICAN rises to his knees, pulls scarf from his sack, puts it on.)

OVERSEER: Now, hold on just a minute! You stop, or I'll…I'll call the Master!

CATO & AFRICAN: Kana kali…maneka macombe…sihana saluke! Kana kali…maneka macombe…sihana saluke!

(SOUND: trumpet call offstage. AFRICAN rises to his feet, begins dancing. MUSIC: African drumming.)

CATO: Fly to Freedom, my brother! Fly! Fly!

AFRICANS: Fly! Fly! Fly! Fly! Fly! Fly! Fly! Fly!

OVERSEER: I said, no flying! You gotta stop! Master! Master!

(SOUND: trumpet call offstage. MUSIC: African drumming crescendos. AFRICAN dances/flies offstage left.)

CATO: Kana kali…maneka macombe…sihana saluke! Kana kali…
maneka macombe…sihana saluke!
AFRICANS: Kana kali…maneka macombe…sihana saluke! Kana kali…
maneka macombe…sihana saluke! Kana kali…maneka macombe…
sihana saluke! Kana kali…maneka macombe…sihana saluke!

(AFRICANS and CATO continue chant as each AFRICAN puts on scarf and dances/flies around stage. MASTER enters from left with a pistol in his hand.)

OVERSEER: I told 'em to stop, but they wouldn't!
MASTER: You don't *tell* a slave to stop. You just stop him!
AFRICANS: Kana kali…maneka macombe…sihana saluke! Kana kali…
maneka macombe…sihana saluke!

(MASTER fires pistol at flying AFRICANS; they are unhurt and fly past him and OVERSEER offstage left. Drumming, chanting stop.)

MASTER: *(points to CATO)* That one there is trouble. Tie him up!

(OVERSEER goes to CATO and attempts to pull his arms behind his back, but CATO flings him away and dons scarf.)

CATO: *(laughs)* I feel sorry for you. Sorry for your ignorance. You know
not the power of the soul. The power of the trumpet's call. The power
of Freedom and the power of man and woman to fly to it.
OVERSEER: Sassy old feller, ain't he?
CATO: Kana kali…maneka macombe…sihana saluke!
MASTER: You quit that crazy talk! *(points pistol at CATO)* Hear me!

(SOUND: trumpet call offstage. MUSIC: African drumming.)

CATO: Kana kali…maneka macombe…sihana saluke!

(CATO dances/flies offstage left. Drumming continues at low volume.)

MASTER: Well, I guess you better tend to the harvest, son.
OVERSEER: But I saw…you saw…they…they flew—
MASTER: I saw nothing of the kind. A trick of the light…fever…this
damned heat will be the death of us all.
OVERSEER: But they…they…I saw—

MASTER: You saw *nothing*. And you will say *nothing*. Not a word about this to anyone—*ever!*

(MASTER prods OVERSEER ahead of him, exiting left.)

SLEEPY JOHN: But despite the wishes of the man who called himself Master, the tale got told. Told a hundred times. A thousand times. A hundred thousand times and more. Told just like I'm telling you now. And it's got to keep on being told. Told everywhere a person is made to bend their back against their will and suffer the pain of the whip, just because someone calls them "slave." *(plays a riff on guitar)* Time for me to move along. Now it's your turn to do the tell.

(He begins playing "Where Shall I Be When the First Trumpet Sounds?" on guitar as EIGHT AFRICANS, CATO and RACHEL enter and sing as chorus.)

CHORUS:
Where shall I be when the first trumpet sounds?
Where shall I be when it sounds so loud?
Sounds so loud, till it wake up the dead
Where shall I be when it sounds?

Where shall I fly when the first trumpet sounds?
Where shall I fly when it sounds so loud?
Sounds so loud, till it wake up the dead
Where shall I fly when it sounds?

Where shall I pray when the first trumpet sounds?
Where shall I pray when it sounds so loud?
Sounds so loud, till it wake up the dead
Where shall I pray when it sounds?

Where shall I be when the first trumpet sounds?
Where shall I be when it sounds so loud?
Sounds so loud, till it wake up the dead
Where shall I be when it sounds?

(MUSIC ENDS; LIGHTS OUT.)

THE END

Where Shall I Be When the First Trumpet Sounds?

(traditional, arranged by L.E. McCullough)

Where shall I be when the first trum- pet sounds?

Where shall I be when it sounds so loud? When it

sounds so loud, till it wake up the dead

Where shall I be when it sounds?

Go Down, Hannah

(traditional, arranged by L.E. McCullough)

Why don't you go down old Han-nah? Well, well, well Don't you rise

no mo- re Don't you rise no mo- re Why don't you go down old

Han- nah- -ah Han- nah Don't you rise no more

Hey, Rattler, Hey

(traditional, arranged by L.E. McCullough)

When I first come o-ver a- cross the sea   Hey, ratt- ler, hey

Come to the land of li- ber- ty   Hey, ratt- ler, hey   All I see is

folks in chains   Hey, ratt- ler, hey Spend their life in fear and pain

Hey, ratt- ler, hey Well, it's   hey, hey, ratt- ler   Hey, ratt- ler,

hey Well, it's   hey, hey, ratt- ler   Hey, ratt- ler, hey

THE SEVEN CHAN BROTHERS OF PAIUTE PASS

The Seven Chan Brothers of Paiute Pass is based upon an ancient Chinese tale recast in a New World setting. In the Old World tale, the brothers resisted the tyranny of a corrupt, oppressive prince; here, they struggle against the blatant anti-foreigner discrimination that flared frequently in the early days of the American frontier—particularly on occasions when large sums of money were at stake. In both versions, Good triumphs over Evil not by heroic feats of battle but by depending upon the confident strength of one's inner being, thus influencing external forces and even nature itself on behalf of the honest, truth-seeking person.

TIME: 1892; The Present

PLACE: Paiute Pass, northwestern Colorado in the heart of the Rockies

CAST: Cap Weaver   7 Chan Brothers
       Brad   Widow Flaherty
       Brittany   Mine Foreman Horvay
       Bartender   Sheriff Hobb
       Barmaid   2 Deputies
       Piano Player   2 Gamblers
       Prospector   Hangman

STAGE SET: three scrims or background curtains can be painted to suggest a ghost town and abandoned mine (stage right), a saloon interior (center) and a rural scene in China (stage left); saloon set has a bar, table, two chairs, a sign reading "Barking Buffalo"; ghost town set has a barrel at down right and a hand-painted sign reading "Paiute Pass, Col."

PROPS: map; tour book; 2 bags of silver; drinking glass; Mickey Finn powder; pick; foreman's notebook; arrest warrant; noose; dollar bills; electric chair; handkerchief; small rock; money purse

SPECIAL EFFECTS: amplified, reverberating wailing; sound of floodwater rushing, pounding, gushing; wind whistling; electric chair sparks

MUSIC: *Way Out in Colorado; Song of the Four Seasons;* piano player can play snatches of background and narrative music throughout ("silent movie music"), interacting with the cues for Chinese music, which can be variations of the *Song of the Four Seasons* played on flute, recorder, violin or other solo melody instuments.

131

COSTUMES: Brad and Brittany wear present-day sports clothes; other characters dress in late 19th-century Western mining camp garb—Sheriff and Deputies have badges, pistols and gunbelts; Barmaid, Bartender, Gamblers, Piano Player and Widow Flaherty wear costumes appropriate to their social station; Hangman dresses in somber black suit and hat; Cap Weaver and Foreman Horvay in plaid shirt, suspenders, jeans, work boots; Seven Chan Brothers wear silk robes, similar perhaps to contemporary Asian martial arts outfits

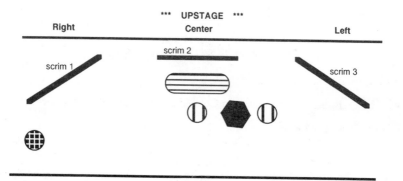

Stage Plan —*The Seven Chan Brothers of Paiute Pass*

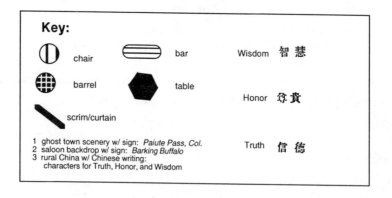

(LIGHTS UP. At stage right CAP WEAVER, an old prospector type, sits on a barrel outside a scrim depicting a dilapidated shack that has an old hand-painted sign—"Paiute Pass, Col."—hanging from it. He is polishing a small rock and humming "Way Out in Colorado." Two teenagers— BRAD, carrying a map, and BRITTANY, carrying a tour book—enter from left. They walk to center stage looking at BRAD'S map, scratching their heads, pointing in various directions; BRITTANY spots CAP WEAVER.)

BRITTANY: There's somebody. Let's ask him how to get back to the interstate.

BRAD: Look, Brittany, I *know* where we are. Or, pretty close to where we are.

BRITTANY: Brad, we have been driving around for an hour since you decided to take the *(makes quote gesture)* "short cut" back at Gypsum.

BRAD: Are you implying I'm lost?

BRITTANY: No, darling, but it would be nice to get to the ski lodge before the next century.

CAP WEAVER: *(clears throat)* Ahem. Help you folks?

BRAD: Nahhh—

BRITTANY: Yes, thank you. *(crosses to CAP WEAVER pulling BRAD behind her)* We were headed for Steamboat Springs and—

CAP WEAVER: Steamboat Springs? Whoa, you're way off track, young lady.

BRITTANY: Where exactly are we, sir?

CAP WEAVER: Excuse my manners; we don't get many visitors. *(tips hat)* Cap Weaver's the name. *(points to sign above him)* And you're in Paiute Pass, Colorado. Used to be the biggest silver mine in the Rockies.

BRAD: *(fumbles with map)* Doesn't seem to be on the map.

CAP WEAVER: *(chuckles)* Oh, no, sonny, you won't find it there. Paiute Pass has been off the map for over a century. First came the boom— over ten thousand miners in six months while the ore lasted. Then the lode played out, and overnight came the bust. Every soul who could swing a pickax ran off to the next strike—Gizzard Gulch, Bird-shot Canyon, Fiddletown, Dead Broke, Strawberry.

BRITTANY: So this is like a "ghost town"?

BRAD: What a cool theme park! Hey, I love the old prospector getup. Where are the rides and stuff?

The Seven Chan Brothers of Paiute Pass 133

CAP WEAVER: *(chuckles)* It's a tour you want, eh? Sure, I'll show you some sights. Follow me.

(He stands and points to center stage where a BARTENDER, BAR-MAID, PIANO PLAYER and TWO GAMBLERS playing cards have entered and take their positions at the bar under a florid sign reading "Barking Buffalo." MUSIC: piano player plays "Way Out in Colorado," sung by BARTENDER, BARMAID and TWO GAMBLERS.)

CHORUS: *(sing)*
Hooray for Colorado where the gold and silver flow
There's plenty of ore and riches galore beneath the peaks of snow
Way out in Colorado, we're comin' to Colorado
With a four-horse team we'll soon be seen way out in Colorado

CAP WEAVER: Back in 1892, the silver practically jumped up out of the ground and chased after a man. Somebody struck it rich in Paiute Pass nearly every day.

(PROSPECTOR enters from right and strides to center, brandishing a bag of silver in each fist.)

PROSPECTOR: Euuuuuu-reka! Drinks on the house! I have hit the mother lode!

BARMAID: Better watch out it don't hit back.

(She snickers and nods to BARTENDER, who winks in acknowledgement.)

PROSPECTOR: *(to BARTENDER)* Gimme the best you got!

BARMAID: *(sidles up to PROSPECTOR)* I'm the best he's got! Jimmy, give this gent the Barking Buffalo special!

BARTENDER: You bet, Tulsa!

(BARMAID leads PROSPECTOR to a table, sits him in chair and flirts with him; BARTENDER pours powder into glass, making a "Mickey Finn.")

BARTENDER: One Barking Buffalo on the rocks!

BARMAID: *(serves PROSPECTOR)* Here you go, sweetie. Bottoms up!

(PROSPECTOR drains glass, smiles, frowns, crosses eyes and collapses on table, unconscious.)

BARTENDER & GAMBLERS: Bottoms up!
BARMAID: Hop to it, boys!

(GAMBLERS drag PROSPECTOR offstage left, while BARMAID presents his two bags of silver to BARTENDER.)

BARMAID: Keep this safe till he wakes up.
BARTENDER: *(puts bags behind bar)* Which oughta be next summer?

(BARTENDER and BARMAID cackle and go back to waiting positions at bar.)

CAP WEAVER: Yessirree, once word of the big strike got out, folks came to Paiute Pass from just about everywhere—Europe, Australia, South America, you name it. One day a Chinese fella strolled into the Barking Buffalo.

(CHAN BROTHER #1 enters from left, approaches bar and bows politely to BARTENDER.)

BARTENDER: Laundy's two doors down, Hop Sing.
BROTHER #1: Oh, so sorry, honorable sir. My name not Hop Sing. Name is Chan. And I not looking for laundry. I seek mine. To work in. *(bows)*
BARMAID: You want to work in a mine? *(to BARTENDER)* Sweet sarsparilla, he's been out in the sun too long.
BARTENDER: Friend, this is a white man's town, ever since we run off the last of the Indians. You savvy? They don't hire Chinese to work in the mines. Not to work anywhere, except the laundry. Now, you mosey on outa town the way you come in, and you won't have annnnny trouble.
BROTHER #1: *(bows)* Thank you, honorable sir, honorable madam. Mine is which way?

(SHERIFF HOBB and TWO DEPUTIES enter from left.)

BARMAID: Sheriff Hobb! *(nods head at CHAN)* Chop suey train just pulled in.
SHERIFF HOBB: Here he is, boys. *(to BARTENDER)* We had word a Chinaman was in town.

(BROTHER #1 bows to SHERIFF and DEPUTIES.)

BROTHER #1: Name Chan. Come to work.

BARMAID: He wants to work in a mine.

SHERIFF HOBB: You want to work in a mine?

BROTHER #1: Yes, sir. Work hard. Work fast.

SHERIFF HOBB: Can't. It's illegal: the Chinese Exclusion Act of 1880, passed by both houses of Congress and signed into law by President Rutherford B. Hayes. You ain't even supposed to be allowed in the country, let alone take away jobs from Americans. And if you don't *have* a job, you must be a vagrant. Arrest him, boys, and throw him in the hoosegow.

(TWO DEPUTIES grab BROTHER #1's arms on each side but cannot move him; mine FOREMAN HORVAY enters from left carrying a pick.)

BARMAID: Well, if it ain't Foreman Horvay, the tunneling teetotaler!

FOREMAN HORVAY: A shaft just gave way at the Tipperary Belle! All the crew have quit, and I can't find a single manjack in town willing to dig 'er out and post 'er up again.

BROTHER #1: *(throws off DEPUTIES)* I work in your mine. *(bows)*

FOREMAN HORVAY: *(looks him up and down)* Well, I'm in no position to be choosy. If you can do the job, you're hired. *(hands pick to BROTHER #1)* Three squares and a dollar a day is the stake. You'll have to pay your own funeral. Come on. *(exits right)*

BROTHER #1: *(bows to SHERIFF, DEPUTIES, BARMAID, BARTENDER)* I go work now.

(He walks to the mine set at mid right, as CHAN BROTHERS #2-7 enter from left and stand mid left, stepping forward and miming with descriptions as they are mentioned. MUSIC: "Song of the Four Seasons.")

CAP WEAVER: What Foreman Horvay didn't know—in fact, what nobody in Paiute Pass knew—was that this Chan fella had six brothers. They all lived in China, and even though they looked the same, each one had different amazing powers. Brother Number Two had incredible ears: he could hear a snowflake slide off a tree limb before it hit the ground. Brother Number Three possessed unbelievable sight: he could stand in China and look halfway round the world and count the feathers on a spotted owl in Montana. Brother Number Four was a stocky fella: his body was built like iron. Brother Number Five had legs so long that, when he unfolded them all the way out, he stood tall enough to wade through the Pacific Ocean from one side to the other. Brother Number Six could handle heat like nobody's business, and when Brother Number Seven sneezed or cried, his tears welled up and flooded the land for miles.

(MUSIC ENDS. BROTHERS #2-7 sit, heads down in a meditative position, as BROTHER #1 grabs pick and works; FOREMAN HORVAY and WIDOW FLAHERTY enter from right and point approvingly.)

CAP WEAVER: And Chan Brother One was the strongest: he could tunnel through a granite mountain like it was sand and carry a full team of oxen on his back from here to El Paso without breaking a sweat. In no time at all, he had the fallen mine shaft all shored up, and he turned the Tipperary Belle into the best-producing mine in the state. Widow Flaherty and Foreman Horvay were mighty proud, and it looked like the hardluck Widow might see some blue skies after all.

WIDOW FLAHERTY: I don't know where you found him, but he's the best miner I've ever seen. Works day in, day out, all through the night without a word of complaint. And he's so polite.

(BROTHER #1 smiles and bows; WIDOW FLAHERTY curtseys.)

BROTHER #1: Confucius say, "Happy is the man who seeks all that he wants in himself. Man who seeks from others is forever unhappy." *(goes back to work)*

FOREMAN HORVAY: *(checking his notebook)* We've had a good haul this month, ma'am. Another week or two, and you'll be able to pay off your mortgage and save your home from foreclosure by the bank.

WIDOW FLAHERTY: And save the Tipperary Belle Mine. It was all my late husband Martin left me. I wish he could see how it's panning out now.

(SHERIFF HOBB and TWO DEPUTIES enter from left, stride across stage and confront the WIDOW and FOREMAN HORVAY; the SHERIFF holds a warrant.)

SHERIFF HOBB: Ma'am, you've got a felon on your premises.

WIDOW FLAHERTY: A felon! That's no way to talk about yourself, Sheriff. *(she and HORVAY laugh)*

SHERIFF HOBB: It's no joking matter. Your man Chan stole a horse last night down by Gizzard Gulch.

FOREMAN HORVAY: It's a lie! Chan wouldn't steal a breath of air that didn't belong to him. He hasn't even been off our property since he got here.

SHERIFF HOBB: *(points to DEPUTIES)* These two citizens caught him in the act.

(DEPUTIES nod and tip their hats.)

DEPUTY #1: Saw him yellow-handed.

DEPUTY #2: Swear on a stack of Bibles.

WIDOW FLAHERTY: You're the thieves! You want to steal the Tipperary Belle for the crooked bankers that own your soul!

SHERIFF HOBB: Tell it to the judge. Bring him along.

(DEPUTIES handcuff BROTHER #1 and march him off to center stage where BARTENDER stands as JUDGE, BARMAID and TWO GAMBLERS as JURY.)

BARMAID & TWO GAMBLERS: Guilty as charged!

BARTENDER: To be hung by the neck until utterly deceased!

(BARTENDER, BARMAID, SHERIFF and TWO GAMBLERS exit behind center scrim; TWO DEPUTIES remain and guard BROTHER #1, who sits on the floor in lotus position and meditates. MUSIC: "Song of the Four Seasons" played on flute under dialogue.)

WIDOW FLAHERTY: *(cries)* The poor innocent man! Is there no justice in the world? Is there no one who can save him?

(BROTHER #2 awakes and hears WIDOW FLAHERTY crying; he awakens BROTHER #3.)

BROTHER #2: Brother, brother! Someone is crying! They are so sad! Can you tell who it is?

BROTHER #3: *(looks around)* Yes, it is an old woman across the ocean in America.

BROTHER #2: America! That is where our baby brother Chan has gone to work. Do you see him?

BROTHER #3: *(stands, peers intently)* Yes, yes, I see him! Oh no, brother! Oh no!

BROTHER #2: What is it?

BROTHER #3: Our baby brother is in great difficulty! Some very bad men have captured him.

BROTHER #2: Let me listen. *(stand, listens)* Yes, yes, they are going to hang him tomorrow at dawn!

(BROTHER #4 awakes and rises.)

BROTHER #4: I will go and save him! They will not be able to hang me, for I am strong like iron!

BROTHER #3: Then go, Brother Chan, and fly like the wind!

(MUSIC changes to wild improvisations of "Song of the Four Seasons." BROTHER #4 rises and dances/whirls his way across stage, ending up at center where he sneaks past the two sleeping DEPUTIES and changes places with BROTHER #1, who hugs him and exits right. BAR-TENDER, BARMAID, SHERIFF and TWO GAMBLERS re-enter from behind scrim and face audience, forming a semicircle around BROTHER #4. FOREMAN HORVAY and WIDOW FLAHERTY stand off to right, heads bowed, as a HANGMAN enters from left and saunters to center swinging a noose. Music stops.)

HANGMAN: Hear there's a job for me this mornin'.

BARMAID: Would you care for a libation?

HANGMAN: What do you take me for, missy? A professional don't imbibe on the job! *(tickles her under chin)* Though we might maybe could share a whiskey or ten after I'm done workin'…

SHERIFF HOBB: *(to DEPUTIES)* Prepare the prisoner for execution of sentence.

(MUSIC: macabre gallows piano music. DEPUTIES present a smiling, bowing BROTHER #4 to HANGMAN who puts noose around his neck. DEPUTIES stand BROTHER #4 on chair. HANGMAN pulls noose tight. BROTHER #4, smiling and nodding, jumps off chair and falls to knees. Music stops; crowd gasps.)

CROWD: Gasp!

(BROTHER #4 smiles and stands up, bows to HANGMAN, SHERIFF, DEPUTIES.)

BROTHER #4: "He who overcomes others is strong, but he who overcomes himself is mightier still." Lao Tzu. *(bows)*

HANGMAN: Great leapin' Lucifer! Thirty years in the hangin' business, and this is the first time I ever lost a client. I mean, first time I *didn't* lose one! *(to BARMAID)* They don't usually smile after I hang 'em.

SHERIFF HOBB: *(feels BROTHER #4's shoulders and chest)* Why, he's made outa iron!

HANGMAN: *(feels BROTHER #4's neck)* Somebody shoulda told me this before we started! There won't be no hangin' this fella! *(to SHERIFF)* I, ahem, still to receive payment for my services.

BARTENDER: What'll we do, Sheriff? Let him loose?

SHERIFF HOBB: *(pays HANGMAN)* Not while there's a law that says a condemned Chinaman has to be killed, one way or another.

DEPUTY #1: Is there a law like that?

SHERIFF HOBB: Don't matter. I'm the law in Paiute Pass, and I say we throw him into the Little Snake River and drown him, tomorrow at dawn.

BARMAID: All in favor, buy a drink at the bar!

(SHERIFF, TWO GAMBLERS, HANGMAN step to the bar and order drinks, then retire with BARTENDER behind scrim as TWO DEPUTIES sit at table and guard BROTHER #4, who sits on floor in lotus position and meditates. MUSIC: "Song of the Four Seasons" played on flute under dialogue.)

BROTHER #3: Brothers, gather! We have a problem!

(BROTHERS #2, 5, 6 and 7 gather around him.)

BROTHER #2: Let me listen. *(listens)* Aaaahhh, our beloved fourth Brother has succeeded in freeing our beloved Brother Number One!

(BROTHERS cheer.)

BROTHER #2: But he is now himself a prisoner.

BROTHER #7: A prisoner! Ohhhhhh…

(BROTHER #7 begins to sniffle; BROTHERS #2, 3 and 6 struggle to restrain him.)

BROTHERS #2, 3 & 6: Brother, no! Do not cry, please!

(BROTHER #5 steps forward.)

BROTHER #5: Brothers, I will save our esteemed fourth Brother! They can throw me from their highest mountain into their deepest river, but I will not be harmed!

(BROTHER #7 sighs with relief and BROTHERS #2, 3 and 6 release him.)

BROTHER #3: Then go, Brother Chan, and fly like the wind!

(MUSIC changes to wild improvisations of "Song of the Four Seasons." BROTHER #5 dances/whirls his way across stage, ending up at center where he sneaks past the two sleeping DEPUTIES and changes places with BROTHER #4, who hugs him and exits right. BARTENDER, BARMAID, SHERIFF, HANGMAN and TWO GAMBLERS re-enter from behind scrim and face audience, forming a semicircle around BROTHER #5. FOREMAN HORVAY and WIDOW FLAHERTY come to center and join crowd. Music stops.)

FOREMAN HORVAY: Sheriff Hobb, the Widow Flaherty wants to have a word with you.

WIDOW FLAHERTY: *(steps forward, offering purse of money)* I don't have much money left, but I want to offer the pittance I have to pay for that young man's freedom.

DEPUTY #2: Sounds like bribery, Sheriff.

DEPUTY #1: Ain't that against the law?

DEPUTY #2: Only if the offer's too low.

WIDOW FLAHERTY: *(kneels)* I'll sign the mine deed over to the bank! Anything...anything to save the life of an innocent man!

SHERIFF HOBB: Madam, you're a day late and a dollar short. This boy has a date with destiny! Deputies, take him to the gorge!

(DEPUTIES and GAMBLERS take BROTHER #5 to down center as saloon crowd stands behind.)

GAMBLER #1: See all that water down there? That's the Little Snake River. Two thousand feet straight down. *(whistles, mimics falling motion with hands)*

BROTHER #5: *(smiles)* That is a very pretty river. It reminds me much of the river that runs by our home in China.

GAMBLER #2: Well, maybe you can sprout wings and fly there. *(laughs)*

SHERIFF HOBB: Haul aweigh, boys!

(DEPUTIES and GAMBLERS heave BROTHER #5 off cliff; he leaps, tumbles, whirls but lands on his feet, bows.)

WIDOW FLAHERTY: St. Patrick be praised, he's still standing!

FOREMAN HORVAY: It's like he grew a hundred feet tall!

BARTENDER: He's still alive! It's impossible!

BROTHER #5: It is the unchanging Tao, sir. Tao is a great square with no angles, a great vessel that never empties, a great sound that cannot be heard, a great sight that can never be seen.

BARMAID: Am I the only one around this town thinking there's something awful fishy about this Chinaman?

DEPUTY #1: We couldn't hang him.

DEPUTY #2: We couldn't drown him.

SHERIFF HOBB: Then we'll burn him!

(CROWD stares at BROTHER #5, then SHERIFF.)

SHERIFF HOBB: There's this new contraption they invented back East a couple years ago. It's called "an e-lectric chair." Tried it out on a prisoner in New York in 1890.

GAMBLER #1: What's this e-lectric stool do?

SHERIFF HOBB: Chair. E-lectric chair. Well, it's real simple, folks. The condemned—

(CROWD looks at BROTHER #5, who smiles and bows.)

SHERIFF HOBB: —sits in the chair. Which is connected to an e-lectric current. Switch gets thrown, current warms the chair nice and toasty, and in just a few minutes…you've got cooked filet of Chinaman.

GAMBLER #2: Sounds like the Tuesday lunch special here at the Barking Buffalo.

SHERIFF HOBB: Deputies, take the prisoner back to jail.

HANGMAN: Where do you get one of these e-lectric saddles, Sheriff?

SHERIFF HOBB: Chair, I said chair. For the last cotton-pickin' time, it's an e-lectric *chair!* Not a stool, not a saddle, not a shoeshine stand—a chair! With a seat guaranteed to fry the britches off the Devil himself!

(CROWD returns behind scrim. BROTHER #5 sits on floor in lotus position while DEPUTIES bring in an electric chair, chuckle, then sit in bar chairs and drowse. MUSIC: "Song of the Four Seasons" played on flute under dialogue.)

BROTHER #7: *(to BROTHER #2)* Brother Chan, what do you hear from across the sea?

BROTHER #2: *(listens)* Alas, our most gracious fifth Brother has been apprehended in the act of assisting Brother Number Four!

BROTHER #3: *(stares toward center)* And they are transporting some kind of sitting device.

BROTHER #6: A rickshaw?

BROTHER #3: Perhaps. But with strings of fire! Brothers, they are going to burn our loyal fifth Brother!

BROTHER #7: Burn him? Ohhhhhhh…

(BROTHER #7 begins to sniffle; BROTHER #6 stops him.)

BROTHER #6: Wait! That must not be! I will go to this wicked place and save him!

BROTHERS #2, 3 & 7: Hurrah for Brother Chan!

BROTHER #6: White-hot flames can lick my skin from head to toe, but they are as the gentle caress of a kitten's tongue.

(MUSIC changes to wild, improvisations on "Song of the Four Seasons." BROTHER #6 dances/whirls his way across stage, ending up at center where he sneaks past the two sleeping DEPUTIES and changes places with BROTHER #5, who hugs him and exits right. BARTENDER, BARMAID, SHERIFF, HANGMAN and TWO GAMBLERS re-enter from behind scrim and face audience, forming a semicircle around BROTHER #6; FOREMAN HORVAY and WIDOW FLAHERTY have moved to the right. DEPUTIES put BROTHER #6 into electric chair. Music stops.)

SHERIFF HOBB: By the authority vested in me by the state of Colorado—

WIDOW FLAHERTY: And your own cold, evil heart!

SHERIFF HOBB: I hereby declare the condemned to pay his full debt to society.

FOREMAN HORVAY: A society of criminals!

SHERIFF HOBB: *(motions to HANGMAN holding switch)* Light 'er up, McDuff!

(MUSIC: fierce, driving piano music. HANGMAN throws switch, STAGE LIGHTS FLICKER, sparks/flames shoot out of electric chair; LIGHTS UP FULL, CROWD gasps, music stops.)

CROWD: Gasp!

WIDOW FLAHERTY: Innocence wills out!

(BROTHER #6 rises from electric chair, dusts himself off, bows, smiles.)

BROTHER #6: Thank you for your hospitality. I had always heard America was a very warm place. *(bows, moves to exit right)*

SHERIFF HOBB: Not so fast.

(DEPUTIES grab BROTHER #6.)

BARTENDER: What in the world are you gonna do with this Chan feller, Sheriff?

SHERIFF HOBB: Well, if he won't hang and won't fall and won't burn …we're gonna just have to shoot him! Deputy, call the Governor and see if the Army will loan us a Gatling gun and a couple of artillery pieces, oh, about yea big.

BROTHER #3: Oh, no! They still restrain our Brother!

BROTHER #7: We must all go and try to save him!

BROTHER #2: We may all die!

BROTHER #3: So be it then! It is but a small thing to lose one's life…it is a serious matter to lose one's virtue.

BROTHER #7: Follow me!

(MUSIC changes to wild improvisations on "Song of the Four Seasons." BROTHERS #2, 3 and 7 dance/whirl their way across stage, ending up at center where they confront the surprised CROWD. From right, BROTHERS #1, 4 and 5 enter and join their BROTHERS at center, gathered around BROTHER #6. Music stops.)

HANGMAN: Well, I thought I'd seen everything! There's seven of these Chan fellers!

GAMBLER #1: *(rubs his eyes)* And they all look exactly alike!

GAMBLER #2: I wonder if they're *real* twins or just pretending so they can get hired by Buffalo Bill's Wild West Show.

SHERIFF HOBB: I don't care if they're the seven brothers for seven brides, we'll shoot every danged one of 'em!

(BROTHER #7 steps forward and begins sniffling; BARMAID pulls a handkerchief from her blouse and offers it.)

HANGMAN: What's wrong with him?

BARTENDER: Looks like he's...like he's gonna cry.

BROTHER #1: No! Anything but that!

SHERIFF HOBB: *(shakes his head in disgust)* Foreigners!

BARMAID: Well, it's sort of an emotional moment, ain't it, Sheriff?

BROTHER #1: *(to BROTHER #7)* Brother, perhaps this is not the best time to express your feelings. Remember, one does not drag the lake to catch the moon in the water.

WIDOW FLAHERTY: *(pats BROTHER #7's shoulder)* Go on and cry, you poor gossoon. Go on and cry for all the evil in the world spawned by ignorance and hate. Cry until the stars in the sky are stained with the salt of your tears. Cry till the heavens echo with the sound of your weeping and the sound of sin and sinners washing away from the earth's tortured flesh. Cry!

(BROTHER #7 cries louder and louder; his BROTHERS gather around him as the others back away and begin running offstage. SOUND EFFECT: amplified, reverberating wailing, sound of floodwater rushing, pounding, gushing. LIGHTS OUT, CHAN BROTHERS move to original position at mid left. LIGHTS UP RIGHT on BRAD and BRITTANY, who rise somewhat disoriented.)

CAP WEAVER: *(o.s.)* Oh, that Seventh Brother cried a flood of tears all right. A flood even the old-timers said they'd never seen the like of. Washed through the whole valley, some say even came near to putting Pike's Peak under water...when things finally dried up, Paiute Pass was just a bunch of busted-up sticks...not a single person left...no trace at all of the Tipperary Belle mine.

(LIGHTS UP LEFT on CHAN BROTHERS, who shake hands with each other and bow to audience.)

CAP WEAVER: *(o.s.)* And those Chinese fellas, folks say Brother Number Seven swooshed 'em all the way back across the Pacific to Shanghai, where they enjoyed a lot more adventures.

(LIGHTS OUT LEFT. BRAD and BRITTANY look around, move toward center.)

BRAD: That's weird. The tour dude was here a minute ago.

(MUSIC: ghostly piano music and Chinese flute.)

BRITTANY: *(leafs through book)* What did that man say his name was?

BRAD: I don't know. Hap or Pap something. What's that book you've got?

BRITTANY: *(reads from book)* "*Legends of the West.* The famous Tipperary Belle mine of Colodado, believed to contain vast amounts of buried silver, was discovered by Captain Thomas Weaver in 1897. Weaver, however, was not to enjoy his windfall, as he died serving in the Spanish-American War the following year. The secret of the mine's whereabouts went with Weaver to his grave."

(CAP WEAVER'S echoing voice sings the first line of "Way Out in Colorado" from offstage.)

CAP WEAVER: *(o.s., sings)*

Hooray for Colorado where the gold and silver flow . . .

BRAD: You know, we really ought to try and get to the ski lodge before dark.

BRITTANY: We can look for that mine any old time.

BRAD: Yeh, a few tons of buried silver shouldn't be hard to find.

BRITTANY: Let's boogie!

(BRAD and BRITTANY scurry offstage left. MUSIC: a quick few bars of "Song of the Four Seasons" followed by Chorus offstage singing "Way Out in Colorado.")

CHORUS: *(o.s., sings)*
> Hooray for Colorado where the gold and silver flow
> There's plenty of ore and riches galore beneath the peaks of snow
> Way out in Colorado, we're comin' to Colorado
> With a four-horse team we'll soon be seen way out in Colorado

(SOUND: wind whistling, mixing with Chinese flute music. LIGHTS FADE OUT.)

BROTHER #1: *(o.s.)* Though the white gem be cast into the dirt, its purity cannot be sullied. Though the good man live in a vile place, his heart cannot be depraved. As the fir and cypress withstand the rigors of the winter, so true wisdom is safe in difficulty and danger.

THE END

Song of the Four Seasons
(traditional, arranged by L.E. McCullough)

Way Out in Colorado

(traditional, arranged by L.E. McCullough)

Hoo- ray for Co- lo- ra- do where the gold and sil- ver

flow There's plen- ty of ore and rich- es ga- lore be- neath the peaks

of snow Way out in Co- lo- ra- do, we're co- min' to Co- lo-

ra- do With a four- horse team, we'll soon be seen, way out in Co- lo-

ra- do

THE MOST DANGEROUS WOMAN IN AMERICA

The Most Dangerous Woman in America recounts an adventure from the life of Mary Harris Jones, one of the most extraordinary and heroic figures in American labor history. Known popularly as "Mother Jones," she was born in extreme poverty in rural Ireland in 1830 and immigrated in 1841 to Canada. After her iron molder husband and four children died of yellow fever in Memphis in 1867, Mother Jones devoted the rest of her days (she died in 1930) to helping American workers win fair wages and humane working conditions. She helped organize hundreds of strikes and gave innumerable lectures on behalf of legislation promoting the minimum wage, eight-hour work day and child labor laws. Jailed and threatened with death scores of times, she never wavered in her struggle to win dignity and justice for the men and women who built America from the ground up.

TIME: A Slow Tuesday Morning

PLACE: Somewhere in America

CAST:

Old Lady	Judge
Manager	Army Captain
Herrera, a Clerk	3 Goons
Simonson, a Clerk	5 Miners
Dempsey, a Clerk	3 Militiamen
Guitar Joe	Mrs. Dalton
Tom McDade	Timmy Dalton
Senator Kern	Senator Goff

STAGE SET: center and right stage house a fast-food restaurant interior with serving counter, condiment station, table and 2 chairs, a sign reading "Snak Shak"; at up left is a fireplace and two scrims or curtains—a miner's humble cottage—and two barrels at mid left

PROPS: tea dispenser, cup; creamer and sugar packets; straws; napkins; ketchup packets; guitar; black shawl; 3 rifles; fireplace poker; cooking pot; ledger; pen; judge's gavel; notebook; pencil; telegram

MUSIC: *Pie in the Sky*

COSTUMES: Manager and Clerks wear standard fast-food uniforms—white shirts, string ties, black slacks and black baseball caps emblazoned with *S-S*; Old Lady wears a long black dress and hat with veil c. 1920, wire-rim spectacles and knee-length black boots; Guitar Joe dresses in overalls and work boots and carries a guitar; early 20th-century characters dress in period clothes with appropriate class and occupational distinctions

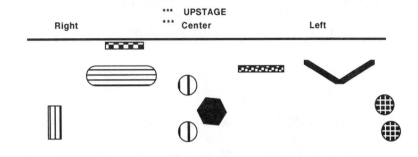

Stage Plan -- *The Most Dangerous Woman in America*

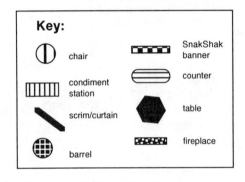

Key:

⬭	chair	▭	SnakShak banner
▥	condiment station	⬭	counter
╱	scrim/curtain	⬡	table
⊕	barrel	▦	fireplace

(LIGHTS UP RIGHT AND CENTER on the interior of Snak Shak, a fast-food chain restaurant. THREE CLERKS stand idly behind the counter; CLERK #2 has only one arm. THE MANAGER enters from stage right and strides to counter; CLERKS immediately snap to attention and make busy work.)

MANAGER: So what is this, a paid holiday? Come on, come on! Let's get busy, people! Let's get busy!

CLERK #1: But, sir, there aren't any customers.

MANAGER: *(steps up to CLERK #1's face)* You know company policy! Snak Shak Handbook, Chapter Four, Section Seven, Paragraph oh-point-one-B-five: "All employees are expected to be involved in productive work *at all times*, regardless of customer service needs or other pre-assigned station duties."

CLERK #2: *(whispers loudly to CLERK #3)* Wonder what kinda production he's involved in?

MANAGER: *(whirls and faces CLERKS #2 and #3)* Someone has a comment?

CLERK #3: I have a request. Next Monday at three-thirty I have a doctor's appointment—

MANAGER: A *what?*

CLERK #3: A…a doctor's appointment. My diabetes, you see, last time the doctor said I should—

MANAGER: There are no excused absences from a scheduled work shift.

CLERK #3: But, I could make it up—

MANAGER: An unexcused absence is the same as stealing. Punishable by termination.

CLERK #3: I was just thinking—

MANAGER: You're not paid to think. Nowhere in your entire Snak Shak training manual are the words "think," "thought" or "thinking" used in relation to an employee.

(AN OLD LADY enters from left and walks up to counter. MANAGER steps to side and CLERK #2 moves forward to wait on the OLD LADY.)

CLERK #2: Welcome to Snak Shak, the tasty top spot in the food chain with twenty-two percent less cases of confirmed food poisoning since 1994.

OLD LADY: Oh, you have such a nice smile. How are you this beautiful morning?

CLERK #2: Gosh, okay I guess. How are you?

OLD LADY: Never felt better. And that's saying a lot at my age. Let's see…I'll just have a cup of tea, if you please. With a smidgen of sugar and a dollop of cream.

CLERK #2: Coming right up. *(calls out)* Tea, cream, sug.

CLERK #1: Tea, cream, sug.

CLERK #3: Tea, cream, sug.

(CLERK #3 pours tea into cup and snaps lid on cup, hands cup to CLERK #1 who puts cream and sugar packets on top of cup and pushes over to CLERK #1 who presents it to the OLD LADY.)

CLERK #2: Here you are.

(MANAGER coughs, folds arms over chest and glares at CLERK #2.)

CLERK #2: Uh, would you like pork fritters to go with that tea?

OLD LADY: Pork fritters? Why no, I don't think so.

CLERK #2: Okay. Eighty-five cents, please.

(OLD LADY hands change to CLERK #2; MANAGER coughs.)

CLERK #2: Uh, we have a special on jalapeño blueberry milk shakes.

(MANAGER coughs.)

CLERK #2: And our deep fried Cajun catfish granola muffins are only forty-nine cents with a side order of tomato-and-tofu cheese wheat paste.

OLD LADY: Goodness gracious, you've got nearly every sort of food there is, don't you? Thanks very much, but I'll just stick to what I came for.

(OLD LADY takes her tea and cream and sugar packets and sits down at the table. MANAGER confronts CLERK #2.)

MANAGER: *(sarcastically)* Good job, Simonson. The average mean sale per transaction figure at this facility is six dollars and thirty-seven cents. According to my latest calculations, you're quite a bit below the mark.

CLERK #2: Yo, man, she only wanted a cup of tea. You want me to shove the food down her throat?

MANAGER: You know, Simonson, when you first came to work here, I thought your *physical* disability might be a problem. I don't think that anymore. I think your chief *handicap*—is your mental attitude. I'm rescinding your morning break. You're on condiment detail. Come on, hustle, hustle, hustle! *(claps hands at each "hustle")*

(CLERK #2 picks up a rag and shuffles, moping, out to condiment station under stern gaze of MANAGER. CLERK #1 timidly approaches MANAGER.)

CLERK #1: Uh, sir, this might not be the best time, but my little boy has been pretty sick lately and missed a lot of school, and I was wondering if I could just spend, like, an hour with him at the hospital.

(points to CLERK #3) Dempsey said he'd take my extra hour and at regular pay and not overtime.

MANAGER: Absolutely out of the question, Herrera. Company policy is explicit on that issue. You don't like it, write your congressman.

CLERK #2: Congressperson.

MANAGER: Simonson! After you've finished condiment detail...*you* can clean the restrooms.

CLERK #2: Yes, *sir!*

MANAGER: I've got a managers' meeting downtown. When I get back, I expect this facility to be in tip-top shape. *(exits right)*

CLERK #2: *(straightens up condiment station and accidentally knocks over some straws)* Dangit! Of all the stupid-stupid-stupid—

OLD LADY: Now there, don't be angry at yourself.

CLERK #2: Huh?

OLD LADY: You're really angry at your manager. And you have every right to be. He's a tyrant and a bully.

(CLERKS #1 and #3 come out from behind counter and listen to OLD LADY.)

OLD LADY: *(chuckles)* Silly man—he thinks he's going to get good workers by abusing them. They just never learn. Why, John D. Rockefeller once told me, "I cheat my sons every time I get a chance. I want to make them sharp." *(chuckles)* Of course, working people in America used to have it worse, but not much. *(To CLERK #3)* How old are you?

CLERK #3: Sixteen.

OLD LADY: A hundred years ago you'd have been likely working in a coal mine. Or a textile mill. Children as young as six and seven worked in the mines as breaker boys. Their task was to sift pieces of slate out of the coal as it poured down long steep chutes in a black, rushing river. Their fingers were cut, broken and crushed. They were beaten routinely by the breaker boss, with no one lifting a finger to stop it. And of the one hundred thousand textile workers in Philadelphia in the early 1900s, sixteen thousand were children, most of them age nine and ten. Most of them with hands cut off, thumbs missing, fingers ripped away at the knuckle, stoop-shouldered and always ill with tuberculosis or pleurisy or pneumonia.

The Most Dangerous Woman in America 153

CLERK #3: Didn't they have laws about all that?

OLD LADY: Oh, yes, the State of Pennsylvania had a law prohibiting anyone under age thirteen from working in an industrial job…but the law was seldom enforced. The children earned two dollars a week and often worked fourteen hours a day. They simply had no choice but to work.

CLERK #1: I know what you mean. I'm a single parent and my ex-husband won't pay his child support. This is the best job I can get.

CLERK #3: I'm saving to go to college. This is the *only* job I can get, and the government keeps talking about lowering the minimum wage. I can barely live on what I make now working full-time!

CLERK #2: But what choice do *we* have? You think the main office of Snak Shak cares about us? We're just expendable parts of a big machine that's going to grind on whether we're part of it or not! *(slaps down towel on condiment station)*

OLD LADY: Friends, you belong to a class which has been robbed, exploited and plundered down through many long centuries. And because you belong to that class, you must fight and help break the chains. That is your *only* choice.

(GUITAR JOE enters from left, carrying an old guitar over his shoulder.)

CLERK #3: Hey, it's Guitar Joe!

GUITAR JOE: Hello, kids!

CLERK #1: *(to OLD LADY)* He's an old street musician comes in for coffee every morning. The manager hates him.

GUITAR JOE: *(sees OLD LADY and beams)* Well, I'll be switched! If it isn't—

OLD LADY: It is, to be sure! And who else would it be? You're looking spry for an old Wobbly, Mr. Hillstrom.

GUITAR JOE: And you, madam! You hold *your* age remarkably well.

OLD LADY: Better than I hold my tongue, no doubt. Give us a song, Joe, and put some fighting spirit into these youngsters!

(GUITAR JOE sings "Pie in the Sky." CLERKS move back to behind counter and OLD LADY walks to stage left as LIGHTS FADE OUT.)

GUITAR JOE: *(sings)*
Politicians come out every night
Try to tell you what's wrong and what's right

But when asked about something to eat
They will answer with voices so sweet

(chorus)
"You will eat bye and bye
In that glorious land in the sky
Work and pray, live on hay
You'll get pie in the sky when you die"

(GUITAR JOE exits right.)

OLD LADY: (o.s.) I turned eighty-two in 1912, and I'd never been busier. In March of that year, I'd helped railway workers in Washington organize against the Pacific Northwest Railroad. In April I'd been in Milwaukee with women workers at a bottling plant. I spent May in Montana with the striking copper miners, and in June I got the news from West Virginia—the bloody Kanawha Valley, where I'd helped the miners organize in 1904, had to be fought all over again. I tied up all my possessions in a black shawl—I liked traveling light—and went immediately.

(LIGHTS UP ON CENTER AND LEFT. OLD LADY is met by TOM McDADE, a union organizer, who enters from left. TWO GOONS sit on barrels at mid left with rifles across their laps.)

TOM McDADE: Greetings, Mother. I'm Tom McDade, United Mine Worker organizer. Welcome to Holly Grove, West Virginia!

OLD LADY: (takes his hand) Thank you. (looks at GOONS) It doesn't seem all that welcome. (pulls McDADE close) What's the situation here?

TOM McDADE: Bad, ma'am. Very bad. When the union asked for an increase from two to two-and-a-half cents per ton, the company fired the union miners and brought in replacements. Those lazy goons you see over yonder are gunmen from the Baldwin-Felts Detective Agency. They've been beating and shooting men and women up and down the valley for a month, and Governor Glasscock won't do a thing to stop it. In fact, he's sending the state militia to support the company.

OLD LADY: The governor is a dirty little coward. He's a lackey for the coal companies, and when they tell him to do their blood work, he orders forth his two faithful generals—Fear and Starvation. One to clutch at the worker's throat and the other at his stomach and the stomachs of his little children. Well, we are not going to surrender.

TOM McDADE: No, ma'am!

OLD LADY: We're going to call a meeting and reorganize the union.

TOM McDADE: Yes, ma'am!

OLD LADY: *(turns to GOONS)* And you can tell him I said so!

(GOONS exit left. MRS. DALTON and TIMMY DALTON have entered from behind scrim; TIMOTHY sits at table, MRS. DALTON tends fireplace. McDADE leads OLD LADY to them, stopping a few feet short.)

TOM McDADE: *(aside to OLD LADY)* You'll be staying with Mrs. Dalton and her son. Her husband was beaten to death last week. They found him at the bottom of the hollow. The company's doctor said he "fell."

(MRS. DALTON turns and greets McDADE and OLD LADY.)

MRS. DALTON: Please come on in. I'm ashamed I have no better accomodation to offer—

(OLD LADY and McDADE step into kitchen, OLD LADY sits at table.)

OLD LADY: Nonsense, my dear. I grew up in the bogs of County Cork in a one-room mud hut. No running water, no windows, the dampness of the earth always present—but a kindly mother and a warm pot of stew on the boil made it seem like a palace to me.

MRS. DALTON: This is my son, Timmy. He'll be eleven next week.

OLD LADY: Hello there, Timmy. What a fine-looking lad you are!

(TIMMY says nothing, turns away.)

MRS. DALTON: I'll go out and get some firewood.

TOM McDADE: I'll give you a hand.

(MRS. DALTON and McDADE exit behind curtain.)

TIMMY DALTON: Ma'am?

OLD LADY: Yes, Timmy?

TIMMY DALTON: What's so special about a union?

OLD LADY: Special? Well, a union is just what it means. Workers united together for a common cause.

TIMMY DALTON: What's their cause?

OLD LADY: To be treated decently by their employers. To work hard and receive honest pay and fair treatment in exchange for their labor. It's the right of every single person in this United States of America.

TIMMY DALTON: My daddy belonged to the union. And they killed him for it. I don't like unions. *(sniffles)*

OLD LADY: Timmy, he didn't die because he joined the union. He died because he refused to let bad men cheat him and treat him wrong. Refused to let them treat you and your mother wrong. Your father died because he wanted a better world for you. A world where you won't have to beg like a dog to live like a man.

TIMMY DALTON: *(sobs)* Mother Jones, please bring my papa back to me! Please!

OLD LADY: *(hugs him)* I can't do that, Timmy. But if we stick together, and fight hard against the cheaters, we can try to make it so no other boys or girls lose their dads.

(TOM McDADE enters.)

TOM McDADE: Ma'am, it's time to set out for the meeting.

OLD LADY: All right. Timmy, you'd better help your mother. You're the man of the house now.

TIMMY DALTON: Yes, ma'am. *(exits behind curtain)*

(GUITAR JOE enters from right, crosses to kitchen table and sings "Pie in the Sky" as FIVE MINERS enter from left and stand in front of scrim and join in on chorus. OLD LADY and McDADE stand in front of barrels.)

GUITAR JOE: *(sings)*
If you fight hard for children or wife
Try to get something good in this life
You're a sinner and bad man, they tell
When you die you will sure go to Hell

GUITAR JOE & MINERS: *(sing)*
You will eat bye and bye (bye and bye)

In that glorious land in the sky (way up high)
Work and pray (work and pray), live on hay (live on hay)
You'll get pie in the sky when you die (that's a lie)

(THREE GOONS enter from left and stand down center, rifles pointed at the gathering.)

GUITAR JOE: *(to audience)* The company, of course, had forbidden the miners to hold meetings. But they came anyway, exercising their first amendment right to peaceably assemble. More hungry, more cold, more starving, more ragged than Washington's army that fought against British tyranny were the miners of the Kanawha Mountains. But just as grim and just as heroic. When the white-haired old woman got up to speak, everything was still. Except for the sight of those guns and the strange, terrified look on everyone's face, no one would know of the bloody war that was raging in those silent hills.

(OLD LADY walks up to one GOON, puts her hand on his rifle muzzle.)

GOON: Take your hand off that gun!

OLD LADY: Young man, I want to tell you that if you shoot one bullet out of this gun at those men, if you touch one of my white hairs, that creek will run with blood!

(GOONS exchange glances, lower rifles, back off. OLD LADY walks back to original position at barrels and addresses miners.)

OLD LADY: You have come over the mountains, twelve, sixteen miles. Your clothes are thin and threadbare…your wives and little ones are cold and hungry…your goodness and patience has cried out to a deaf world. Now you must stop being patient. You must join your brothers all over the state…join the union once more and strike!

MINER: But if we join the union, we'll get fired!

OLD LADY: If you men would just use your brains instead of your mouths! Of every ton of coal you mine, so much is taken out to hire professional murderers to keep you in subjection. You paid for it! You stood there like a lot of cowards and let yourselves be robbed by the mine owners, and then you go about shaking your sad, broken heads. None of these fellows are better than you. They are only flesh and blood. And that is the truth. Join the union, boys! I have been in jail more than once, and I expect to go again. If you are too cowardly to fight, I will fight!

(McDADE holds up a ledger and pen; each MINER walks up and signs. THREE MILITIAMEN enter from left and confront OLD LADY.)

MILITIAMAN #1: You're under arrest for disturbing the peace.

OLD LADY: Is that all? Usually they accuse me of having killed Julius Caesar and cracked the Liberty Bell!

(MINERS exit left; GOONS and MILITIAMEN exit right; GUITAR JOE moves back to counter; JUDGE with gavel enters from left and sits on a barrel, using other barrel as his podium. McDADE and OLD LADY stand to right of Judge.)

TOM McDADE: Good news, Mother. Gene Debs got Clarence Darrow to file a support brief. The judge is suspending your sentence on condition you leave the county immediately.

OLD LADY: What about the miners at the meeting?

TOM McDADE: They got out of jail. But they lost their jobs. Fired, every single one.

JUDGE: *(raps gavel)* You seem to be an intelligent woman, Mrs. Jones, but you have not behaved like a good woman. You have strayed beyond the lines and paths from which the Allwise Father intended your sex to pursue. You are a busybody, madam, who creates dissatisfaction among honest workers. You should devote yourself to charity work in keeping with the true sphere of womanhood.

OLD LADY: Your honor, you are a vile scab, corrupt and rotten to the core. I live wherever there is a fight. I fight for those who can't fight. I am not afraid of the penitentiary, or the scaffold or the sword. I will tell the truth wherever I please. If you want to hang me, then hang me. But when I am on the scaffold, I'll cry "Freedom for the working class!"

JUDGE: May I remind the defendant that she is—

OLD LADY: May I remind the judge that coal is a mineral. No operator, no coal company on the face of the earth made it. It belongs to the nation. It was there down through the ages, and it belongs to every generation that comes along. The story of coal is always the same. It is a dark story. For a second's more sunlight, men must fight like tigers. For the privilege of seeing the color of their children's eyes by the light of the sun, fathers must fight as beasts in the jungle. That life may have something of decency, something of beauty—a picture, a new dress, a bit of cheap lace fluttering in the window—for this, men who work down in the mines must struggle and lose...struggle and win.

JUDGE: *(slams gavel)* You, madam, are the most dangerous woman in America! Leave this courtroom at once! Bailiff!

(JUDGE exits left. McDADE guides OLD LADY to MRS. DALTON'S kitchen where MRS. DALTON is wringing her hands and pacing. McDADE exits left.)

MRS. DALTON: Mother, have you heard? The strike is on! Miners are pouring into Holly Grove from all over the state to show support for our local boys!

OLD LADY: That means the company's bringing in more thugs and gunmen, too. Well, if it's war they want, it's war they'll get.

MRS. DALTON: Do you think we'll ever have peace? The peace to live our lives without threats and intimidation?

OLD LADY: Peace can only be had with justice. The owners seem to think that's too high a cost to pay, so they find it cheaper to make their fellow human beings live like slaves, working on their knees with guns held to their heads. It goes for a while, but injustice boils in men's hearts, as does steel in its cauldron, ready to pour forth, white hot, in the fullness of time.

(McDADE rushes in from left, shirt torn, bloody rag around his head.)

OLD LADY: Good lord, man, what is it?

TOM McDADE: *(gasping)* The guards opened fire on the miners' tents! They've shot over a dozen in cold blood! It's a massacre!

MRS. DALTON: Timmy! *(tries to run past McDADE, who stops her)*

TOM McDADE: No! Don't go out there!

(TWO MINERS enter carrying the dying TIMMY and lay him on table.)

MRS. DALTON: No! *(weeps hysterically)* No!

TIMMY DALTON: *(weakly)* It's...it's okay, ma...I'm gonna...gonna be with pa...in the union...*(dies)*

(An ARMY CAPTAIN and TWO MILITIAMEN enter.)

ARMY CAPTAIN: *(to OLD LADY)* Madam, you are under arrest.

OLD LADY: By whose order?

ARMY CAPTAIN: By order of martial law.

OLD LADY: Fiddlesticks! Charged with what?

ARMY CAPTAIN: Stealing a machine gun, attempting to dynamite a train and conspiracy to commit murder…the penalty for which is death.

(CAPTAIN and MILITIAMEN direct OLD LADY to mid left, where she sits on a barrel. CAPTAIN exits left, MILITIAMEN take up guard position in front of scrim. McDADE, MRS. DALTON, MINERS and TIMMY exit right. LIGHTS FADE DOWN. SPOTLIGHT on OLD LADY, who takes notebook and pencil from her shawl and writes.)

OLD LADY: My Dear Terrence: You have no doubt heard of my arrest by the hounds of capital pirates. They have me in solitary confinement at a military camp near Pratt, West Virginia. Two soldiers guard me day and night. No one is allowed to speak to me, and it is possible this letter will never reach you. I have been suffering from fever …my temperature is a hundred and four…I believe I have pneumonia…God spare me the strength to fight these jackals!

(SPOTLIGHT OUT. LIGHTS UP CENTER on SENATOR KERN and SENATOR GOFF, who stand opposite each other about four feet apart facing toward audience)

SENATOR KERN: I ask my fellow United States Senators to end this reign of terror in our land by sending a congressional commission to investigate the inhuman and unlawful state of affairs in the coal districts of West Virginia—particularly with regard to the illegal imprisonment in a military prison of a private citizen.

SENATOR GOFF: That's preposterous! The Senator from Indiana is severely mistaken! There is no state of emergency in West Virginia! Why, I have been assured that the lady to whom he alludes is being kept in a very delightful, uh, very delightful boarding house. Lots of flowers and tea and such. Delightful.

SENATOR KERN: I must take exception to the Senator from West Virginia. *(pulls out telegram)* I have here a telegram from the lady herself, smuggled out of the prison where she has been incarcerated for over three months without due process of civil law. *(reads)* "To the U.S. Congress: From out the military prison walls in Pratt, West Virginia, where I have been forced to pass the eighty-third milestone of life, I plead with you for the honor of this nation. I am eighty-three years old, and I haven't long to live anyhow. Since I have to die, I would rather die for the cause to which I have given my whole life—if my death would call the attention of the whole United States to conditions in West Virginia. All the world's history has produced no more savage and brutal times than these, and this nation will perish if we do not change these conditions. I send you groans and tears and heartaches of men, women and children as I have heard them in this state, and beg you to force an investigation. Children yet unborn will rise and bless you. Sincerely, Mary Harris Jones."

SENATOR GOFF: Why, that's a fake! The Governor himself told me she was in a boarding house—

SENATOR KERN: Gentlemen of the Senate, I call for a vote!

(LIGHTS OUT. SENATOR GOFF and SENATOR KERN exit left. LIGHTS UP RIGHT AND CENTER on THREE CLERKS and GUITAR JOE at table.)

GUITAR JOE: When the news of Mother Jones' ordeal spread throughout the country and around the world, the authorities were forced to release her. And the Governor of West Virginia signed legislation that ordered the coal companies to grant a nine-hour work day, recognize the United Mine Workers union, give workers the right to organize without fear of intimidation and to shop at other than the company store.

CLERK #1: That's incredible! We're talking one tough old lady! *(looks around.)* Hey, where's she gone?

GUITAR JOE: Wherever she's needed. And that was just one of several hundred union drives she helped organize…literally laying her body on the line, so you kids could have a decent place to work today.

CLERK #3: Yeh, well, this place isn't always so decent.

CLERK #2: But like Mother Jones said, it's up to *us* to change it.

(MANAGER enters from right, glares at GUITAR JOE.)

MANAGER: Oh, it's you again! Freddy the Freeloader! Bug off, wacko!

CLERK #1: *(clears throat, steps forward)* Sir, that's an unacceptable manner of speaking to a customer, no matter what their socio-economic status or estimated mental orientation. If you do so again, I'll have to write you up on report.

MANAGER: Huh?

CLERK #2: Snak Shak Employee Handbook, Chapter Six, Section Three, Paragraph oh-point-one-G-four—

MANAGER: Who told you to talk? Take a toothbrush and scrape out the greasepit!

CLERK #3: *(to CLERK #1)* Ms. Herrera, add that to the grievance list. "Abuse of company personnel assigned to dangerous and unnecessary tasks."

CLERK #1: Yes, sir.

MANAGER: Sir? Hey, who's giving the orders around here?

(CLERKS look at each other.)

CLERK #2: You're not. We've declared your managerial authority suspended, pending review by the district supervisor's committee. And we're also going to file a full report on your conduct violations to our union.

MANAGER: Union! You people don't have a union!

CLERKS #1, #2 & #3: *(link arms, step up to MANAGER)* We do now!

MANAGER: *(backs away right, trembling angrily)* You can't do this! It's unfair! It's un-American! You're all a bunch of troublemakers! Traitors! *(points at GUITAR JOE)* You did this! You and that crazy old lady! *(dashes offstage right)*

CLERK #3: For sure. Old Mother Jones—the most dangerous woman in America.

(CLERKS and GUITAR JOE laugh, shake hands and sing "Pie in the Sky"; SPOTLIGHT LEFT on OLD LADY, standing, smiling, raising fists.)

GUITAR JOE & MINERS: *(sing)*
With the workers of country and town
Mother Jones in the front could be found

She fought for the rights of the poor
For justice and truth ever more

We will eat bye and bye (bye and bye)
In that glorious land beneath the sky (let freedom fly)
Work and pray (work and pray), praise the day (praise the day)
We get pie in the sky before we die (that's no lie)

(LIGHTS OUT.)

THE END

Pie in the Sky

(written by Joe Hill, arranged by L.E. McCullough)